STRONG AS HERCULES

WISE AS ATHENA,

WOMAN

THE GOLDEN AGE

by LES DANIELS

Art Direction and Design by CHIP KIDD

CHRONICLE BOOKS
SAN FRANCISCO

PHOTOGRAPHS
BY GEOFF SPEAR

DESIGN ASSISTANCE
BY CHIN-YEE LAI

Visit DC Comics online at
http://www.dccomics.com
or at keyword DC Comics on America Online.

Library of Congress Cataloging-in-Publication Data
available.
ISBN 0-8118-3123-X  •  Printed in China
Distributed in Canada by Raincoast Books
1050 Shaughnessy Street
Vancouver, British Columbia V6P 6E5
10 9 8 7 6 5 4 3 2 1

Chronicle Books
85 Second Street
San Francisco, California 94105

www.chroniclebooks.com

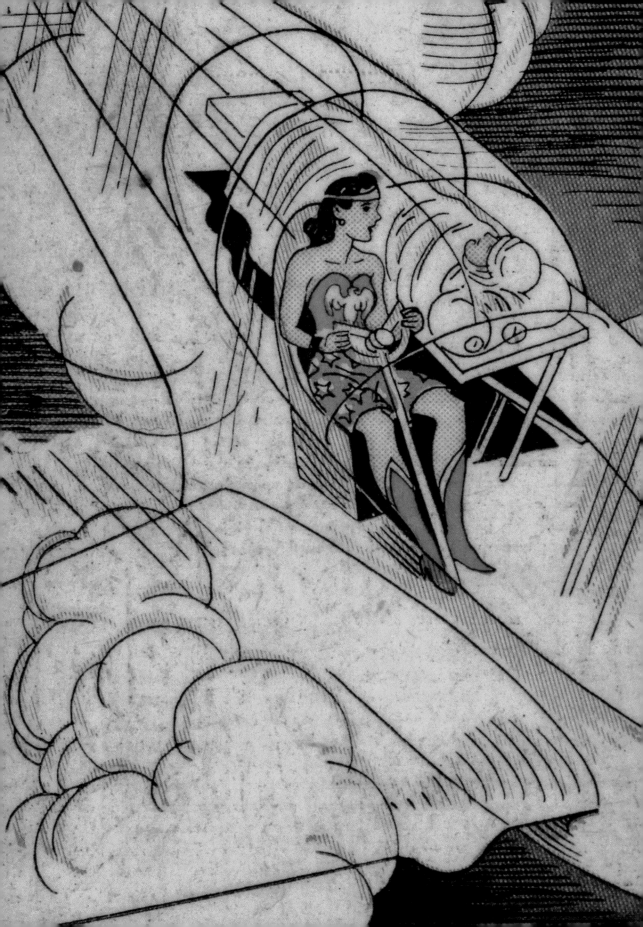

# INTRODUCTION

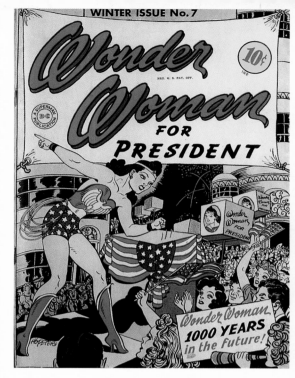

William Moulton Marston, the creator of Wonder Woman, was an extremely accomplished man. He held a doctorate in psychology and a degree in criminal law, and he initiated the development of the systolic blood pressure deception test (lie detector). A prolific writer of many books, periodicals, and magazine articles, he firmly believed in the "natural superiority of women." He truly was a man light-years ahead of his time. Above all, he was my beloved father. He doted on me, his only daughter.

In 1915, he married my mother, Elizabeth Holloway Marston. An exceptionally well educated woman for her time, she held a master's degree in psychology as well as a degree in criminal law. In 1918, my mother was the first woman in the Commonwealth of Massachusetts to pass the bar exam. Many have thought of her as a "wonder woman" in her own right. Her only response was that she was not Wonder Woman but that she was "Wonder Woman's mother."

In the early 1940s, my father was looking for a venue to express his idea of female superiority. The comic strip genre seemed to have far-reaching possibilities. He developed the Wonder Woman character based on the theories he expressed in his book *Emotions of Normal People*. His simplified concept was this: "Force bound by love, love bound by wisdom." All this really means is that if love is properly directed by wisdom ("wisdom thinks"), the force energy will be used to *create,* rather than to destroy.

My father created Wonder Woman during World War II, one of the most tumultuous and destructive periods in the Common Era. The early Wonder Woman stories directly depicted her saving the world from "evil"–i.e., the destructive side of force, in a way that "bound" the evil to see the error of its ways. She demonstrated the natural superiority of women and was meant to be an example of the real power that each woman has inside of her.

William Moulton Marston's vision as paraphrased from one of his own journals was this: Let the vibration of Wonder Woman penetrate the consciousness of all the people on this planet and bring forth the dawn of a new age: the "Golden Age" of Wonder Woman.

I hope it has arrived.

**–Olive Ann Marston LaMotte**

# THE DOCTOR

One of the best known, longest lasting, and most controversial characters in the history of comics, Wonder Woman has always been obliged to play a dual role. In addition to keeping a large audience entertained with her exploits, she has been expected to serve as a representative and an example for her entire gender, and the tension between these two responsibilities has given Wonder Woman a unique

position in America's popular culture. The contradictions were inherent from the time of Wonder Woman's introduction, perhaps because her creator was something of a paradox himself.

In 1941, a Harvard-trained psychologist with a law degree and a Ph.D. assumed a pseudonym and began writing comic books. The medium was new and not held in high regard, hardly the sort of thing expected to occupy the attention of a middle-aged, respected writer who had already acquired a national reputation

In 1938 William Moulton Marston, Wonder Woman's father, posed in a cherry orchard outside the family home in Rye, New York, with his other children (from left): Byrne, Olive, Donn, and Pete.

with his books and articles. Most of Dr. William Moulton Marston's colleagues in comics were young men who had grown up during the Depression with limited access to higher learning, and the upstart industry regarded him as quite a find. "He was a well-educated person," said DC Comics publisher Jack Liebowitz, as if noting an incongruity, "and he wrote his own scripts." Marston's entire comic book output encompassed only a single feature, and that was Wonder Woman.

Marston's ideas were often unconventional, and he was something of a maverick among the psychologists of his day, who were ordinarily safely ensconced in the groves of academe. Although Marston had taught at some of the most respected American colleges and universities, over the years he transformed himself into a consulting psychologist, working to promote his ideas through associations with big business and the entertainment industry. He became a minor celebrity whose name and face were familiar to readers of the popular press, and he was an enthusiastic advocate of new developments in the mass media. Writing in a 1943 issue of *The American Scholar*, a publication of the Phi Beta Kappa society, he explained how he became interested in comic books as an emerging art form:

This phenomenal development of a national comics addiction puzzles professional educators and leaves the literary critics gasping. Comics scorn finesse, thereby incurring the wrath of linguistic adepts. They defy the limits of accepted fact and convention, thus amortizing to apoplexy the ossified

Marston was rare among the intellectuals of his era in accepting the fantastic plots and the image-driven narratives of comic books, at least in part because he thought he saw a chance to do some good. "If children *will* read comics," he asked, "why isn't it advisable to give them some constructive comics to read?" Recognizing the importance of the new breed of super heroes exemplified by Superman, Marston acknowledged that "feeling big, smart, important, and winning the admiration of their fellows are realistic rewards all children strive for. It remains for moral educators to decide what type of behavior is to be regarded as heroic." Marston's answer to that question was embodied in his Wonder Woman stories, one of the most significant bodies of work in the chronicles of his chosen medium. Yet when comic book professionals mention Marston, the first topic of discussion is invariably his status as the man who invented that intriguing device known as the lie detector.

William Moulton Marston was born

arteries of routine thought. But by these very tokens the picture-story fantasy cuts loose the hampering debris of art and artifice and touches the tender spots of universal human desires and aspirations, hidden customarily beneath long accumulated protective coverings of indirection and disguise. Comics speak, without qualm or sophistication, to the innermost ears of the wishful self.

And Marston recognized that the medium might be even more important than the message, in terms of what made comics popular:

It is the *form* of comics-story telling, "artistic" or not, that constitutes the crucial factor in putting over this universal appeal. The potency of the picture story is not a matter of modern theory but of anciently established truth. It's too bad for us "literary" enthusiasts, but it's the truth nevertheless—pictures tell any story more effectively than words.

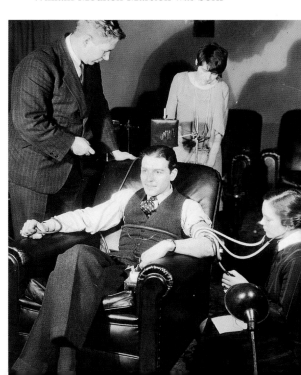

Dr. Marston and assistant Olive Byrne (in back) use the lie detector to test the emotional reactions of an unusually enthusiastic moviegoer.

in 1893 and graduated from Harvard in 1915; later that same year he married Elizabeth Holloway, who had attended Mt. Holyoke. In a letter written more than half a century later to comics fan Jerry Bails, she said that she had been offered a position in her alma mater's psychology department, but she had other plans: "to marry Bill Marston" and "to go to law school, which I also did a week after we were married." She couldn't attend classes with Marston at Harvard, which did not admit women, and she dismissed the era's idea of a separate Harvard law school for women as "lovely law for ladies." Instead, she studied at Boston University and "played around with all the young politicians of the Boston and environs area. Our apartment in Cambridge was a rendezvous for friends from both schools. Bill was a wild mixture but fun." Both Marstons got their law degrees and were admitted to the bar in 1918, but apparently practiced hardly at all. His wife said that Marston had managed to pass his exams without attending classes, because

in 1918 he was doing his part during World War I, serving in the U.S. Army's psychological division, where he rose to the rank of second lieutenant. He received his Ph.D. in 1921 while his wife earned her M.A. degree.

As early as 1915, while an undergraduate studying under Hugo Münster-

# PLEASE BELIEVE ME WHEN I SAY I'M LYING

The lie detector, so closely associated with William Moulton Marston, has been a source of controversy ever since its introduction. Marston's idea was that changes in blood pressure would indicate deception on the part of the subject, and modern versions of the polygraph include a test for sweating palms and a band across the chest to measure changes in breathing. The device may successfully detect an emotional response but can't determine what causes it. Some people experience anxiety just because they're strapped in, while others are agitated by any question that seems to place their integrity in doubt. On the other hand, sociopaths may show no emotion when confronted by their crimes, and some experts indicate that it's possible to beat the test through self-inflicted pain or deliberate changes in breathing. The most objective recent studies seem to suggest that innocent people will often appear guilty.

During World War I, Marston used the device on individuals accused of spying; later, he tested every prisoner in the penitentiaries of Texas. In 1932 he lobbied to test the man accused of the Lindbergh kidnapping, the most sensational crime of its day, but by then the polygraph had been discredited. In the 1923 case *Frye v. United States,* the court ruled that the test had not been accepted by scientists and would be inadmissible. Yet even today police like the lie detector, and defendants who refuse to submit to it may fall under a cloud. The polygraph is also used in business to screen for dishonest job applicants, and even to discover which employees fit Marston's personality types like dominance and compliance. The appeal of an infallible lie detector is obvious, and Marston would create its comic book equivalent in Wonder Woman's golden lasso, which obliges anyone caught in its coils to tell the unvarnished truth.

## The Neglected Wife and Her Roving Husband

**1** **The Complaining Wife** neglected her personal appearance, kissed her husband farewell with no demonstration of affection. She told Dr. Marston her husband neglected her.

**2** **The Husband** went elsewhere for glamour and freely told the psychologist that, without blaming his wife, he felt that he himself was the neglected one.

## Real Life Stories
## From a Psychologist's Files

FROM the field of crime, the "Lie Detector" has entered the fields of love. It now tells whether or not your wife or sweetheart loves you—or you, her. Dr. William Moulton Marston, the inventor, reports success with his device in solving marital or other domestic problems, and adds that it will disclose subconscious secrets of which the subject is utterly unaware. LOOK here presents two actual cases from the famous psychologist's files.

Dr. Marston discovered the principle of lie detection at Harvard in 1915, when he found lying affects breathing and blood pressure. His "detector" is simply an apparatus to measure these changes. An ordinary blood-pressure device is strapped on the leg (see below) and a tube around the chest measures breathing. In the hands of a psychologist these instruments become disinterested truth-finders.

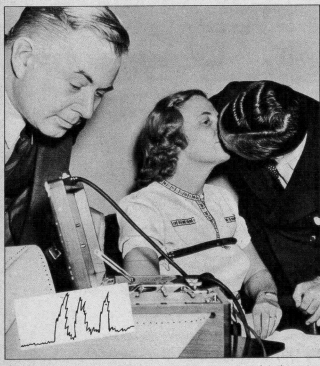

**3** **To Test the Wife's Affections,** Dr. Marston arranged to have an attractive young man kiss her. The graph indicated a strong emotional reaction to the stranger's kiss. The doctor then had to determine how her husband affected her. Before the Lie Detector can be used, the operator must first establish normal graphs, then study deviations.

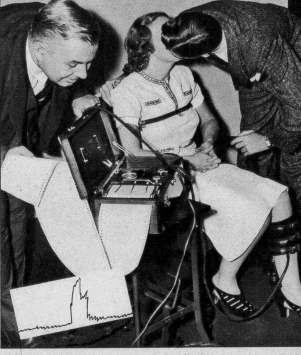

**4** **The Wife's Reaction to Her Husband's Kiss** is tested here. Dr. M ston found (see graph) that she was still fond of him, although showed more pronounced reaction to the other kiss. Dr. Marston belie the marriage could be saved and the couple agreed to try to repair t foundered marriage by showing more consideration for each other.

# Take These Tests?

## The Case of the Boy and the Girl Who Were in Love, But Were Engaged to Others

**Engaged** to a well-to-do, socially promi-nent young man, the girl who came to Dr. Marston was still very unhappy. She told him that she often found solace with a childhood friend, who was, in turn, engaged to the daughter of his employer. Dr. Marston explained to the troubled girl that he first must find her true motives for her present engagement, and asked her to take a lie detector test which would reveal them.

**2 Emotional Upsets** were demonstrated on the graph to two questions asked. The girl said she was really in love with her fiance and that she did not love her childhood friend. But the Lie Detector showed that, although she did not know it, she was wrong in both cases.

**The Childhood Lover** was next tested. The Lie Detector showed that he, too, was still in love, but dared not ask her to marry because he feared he could not support her. Dr. Marston believes course of true love would run much more smoothly if more eption tests were applied in such "triangle cases."

**4 United by the Lie Detector,** the happy couple thank the psychologist, who recommended that they recognize their love and get married. They agreed with him and did. The application of the Lie Detector to lovers' problems is new, but 300 U. S. police departments use it to test suspected criminals. Dr. Marston also has applied his test to determine the honesty of employes.

Dr. Marston even tried to prove the lie detector could be used to solve romantic problems, as demonstrated in this article from *Look* magazine (December 6, 1938).

16

berg, Marston became interested in the detection of deception, and in 1917 he published a paper in *The Journal of Experimental Psychology* called "Systolic Blood Pressure Symptoms of Deception." This seems to have formed the basis for claims that Marston "invented" the lie detector; there is, however, no evidence that any sort of device was specially constructed. According to Marston's son Byrne Marston, himself a physician, "the only thing he had was that he thought the blood pressure would go up if someone was lying. He credited himself; I know there was some controversy as to whether he was the first to know that or someone else. But it was just the idea."

Whatever his contribution, Marston was the lie detector's most enthusiastic advocate and bears substantial responsibility for the test's hold on the public's imagination, despite accumulated scientific evidence that it is not completely reliable. Yet it was part of his effort to remove subjectivity from psychology, to establish a way of discussing personality that was not dependent on literary analogies like Sigmund Freud's use of such mythological figures as Oedipus. Ironically, Marston's own theories of human behavior did not stand the test of time, but their introduction into the Wonder Woman stories he wrote enabled him to become one of the twentieth century's major myth makers.

Marston's psychological theories were outlined in his first book, *Emotions of Normal People* (1928). Attempting to avoid the subjectivity inherent in descriptions of emotional states, Marston sought more objective "elementary behaviour units" in the activities of dominance, compliance, submission, and inducement. These were all power relationships, and reflected Marston's interest in control; he described consciousness in terms of success or surrender. Geoffrey C. Bunn, the academic who has made the most thorough study of Marston's theories, has concluded that, "despite claiming that his 'elementary units' were rigorous scientific categories free of literary meaning, Marston was constantly forced to employ literary language to render them intelligible. Not only was he unable to prevent the political and sexual connotations of dominance and submission from emerging, but he even encouraged them."

By page 300 of his book, in a chapter

Although Wonder Woman is William Moulton Marston's most famous fictional creation, he also wrote a historical novel whose themes make it comparable to his comic book work. Both were inspired by Marston's interest in the ancient world, but Wonder Woman was grounded in myth, while *Venus with Us* (1932) was based on the life of the historical soldier and statesman Julius Caesar, assassinated in 44 B.C. (The title was purportedly Caesar's battle cry.) Marston did his research on the details of daily life in the Rome of two thousand years ago, but the *New York World-Telegram* pinpointed the book's weakness by remarking "it seems that Caesar accomplished his major achievement of conquering the world at such odd times as he was not engaged in conquering the women of Rome." Rife with chapter titles like "Ladies' Night in the High Priest's Palace," the book is basically an erotic romp that attributes all of Caesar's famous deeds to his romantic entanglements. Striving to be sexy while conforming to the censorship of the time, the book bogs down under the weight of passages like this: "His soul was lost in beautiful, palpitating dreams of serving her glorious womanhood forever. . . . Those wonderful feet!"

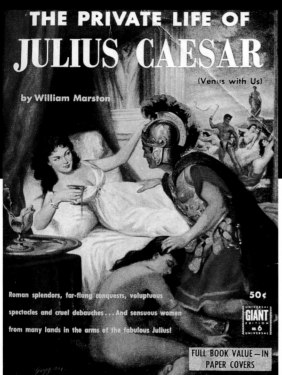

There are also an inordinate number of scenes involving women in bondage, with even Cleopatra showing up in chains for Caesar's delectation. The novel seems to view bygone days as an opportunity to employ all the apparatus of slavery without evoking racism, and one of Caesar's prisoners of war announces "I've only been your slave a short time—but I have a feeling I'm going to like it!" The book was released in a 1953 paperback version as *The Private Life of Julius Caesar*, with one of the era's lurid wraparound covers showing various half-clad women being whipped, chained, and even crucified.

young scholars to these activities, with Marston concluding that "the strongest and most pleasant captivation emotion was experienced during a struggle with girls who were trying to escape from their captivity." And, he added, "it seems probable that the costumes worn by the freshman girls enhanced, considerably, both the passive submission and the active inducement emotions of the upper class girls although great reticence of introspective description, due to conventional suppressions, prevented this type of response from appearing with complete frankness in the reports received." Yet some people say that science is dull!

entitled "Love," Marston was reporting a 1925–1926 study he had conducted with his assistant Olive Byrne on sorority members at Jackson College, the sister school of Tufts. Their subject was the "baby party," a strange sorority ritual in which freshman initiates "were required to dress like babies." They were also bound, blindfolded, and prodded with sticks; when they resisted, wrestling ensued. Four pages of charts documented the responses of the

In a 1928 publicity stunt, duly reported in *The New York Times,* Marston combined the study of his "elementary behaviour units" with the systolic blood pressure test in order to compare the personalities of blondes, brunettes, and redheads. His

William Moulton Marston became recognized as an authority on funny books after this interview with Olive Richard appeared in *The Family Circle* magazine (October 25, 1940).

test subjects were a gaggle of showgirls from Broadway musicals like *Show Boat* and *Rio Rita,* who were hooked up to Marston's equipment so he could gauge their responses to movie footage, including scenes of a dancing slave girl. The stereotyped results suggested that blondes tended toward passivity, while brunettes "enjoyed the thrill of pursuit." The whole affair inspired the cheerful skepticism of the press, who even ungallantly questioned the authenticity of the blondes. Yet Marston was no fool, and was an expert on inducing responses, so he may not have been entirely surprised when at the end of the year his stunt got him a position as a consultant to Universal Pictures.

The job at Universal lasted only a year, but led to Marston's second book, a collaboration with Walter B. Pitkin called *The Art of Sound Pictures* (1930). Pitkin's sections seemed concerned with the carpentry of script construction, while Marston's ranged over a wider field. Among other things, he predicted the use of stereo sound for dramatic impact at a time when mere dialogue was still an innovation, and he foresaw that color photography would become standard although it was still in its experimental stages. He even ran tests on male and female color preference, combined them with blood pressure tests for his four elementary units, and concluded that, for instance, the color blue would inspire feelings of dominance in men but inducement in women, while both genders saw yellow in terms of submission (whether such theories had an effect on the subsequent design of Wonder Woman's costume is anybody's guess).

Marston's study of Universal's output led to high praise for *The Hunchback of Notre Dame,* a very successful 1923 silent

# SHE COULD SEE RIGHT THROUGH YOU

Wonder Woman is often described as the first super heroine, but nothing is as simple as it seems. According to comics historian Will Murray, there is another character who can be considered the first super hero of either sex to get into print, and who is "definitely the first super heroine in comics history!" Even more surprising, this pioneer's publisher later went on to run DC Comics, the place where Wonder Woman eventually found her home.

Harry Donenfeld was a printer, publisher, and distributor who, with his partner Jack Liebowitz, bought the foundering DC Comics from its founder, Major Malcolm Wheeler-Nicholson, in 1938. By then Donenfeld was established, with another partner named Frank Armer, as the purveyor of a line of lurid pulp magazines including *Spicy Mystery Stories* and *Spicy Detective Stories.* Famous for their covers featuring half-dressed women being tied up or otherwise tormented, these periodicals contained short stories with similar embellishments, and also an occasional brief, black-and-white comics story. In its August 1937 issue (four years before Wonder Woman appeared, and almost a year before Superman), *Spicy Mystery Stories* introduced a strip not much longer than its name: "The Astounding Adventures of Olga Mesmer, the Girl with the X-Ray Eyes." Created at a studio run by Adolphe Barreaux, Olga was the daughter of a mad scientist and the mysterious woman who was the victim of his strange experiments. As a result, "she was given super-human strength and the ability to see right thru solid objects." Before long Olga was jumping out of her clothes and bumping off bad guys, but she inadvertently transferred her strength to the hero via a blood transfusion. By October 1938, she'd learned that her mother was from Venus, had taken a trip there, and ended an interplanetary war, but nonetheless Olga never appeared again.

# DON'T LAUGH AT THE COMICS

Everybody has always said it is story value—the primitive thrill of danger and adventure — that makes such strips as "Superman" so popular. But that's not the real reason, says Dr. Marston, Family Circle psychologist, who tells what he thinks it is

WHEN Orson Welles announced in the course of a radio melodrama that octopus men from Mars were invading New Jersey, and people by the thousands believed him, I thought the world had gone mad. It seemed incredible that rational human beings could accept such a fantastic "news announcement" as truth, that they could dash about ringing fire alarms, telephoning hospitals and police, and calling out the National Guard to repel the Martians.

But this is how Dr. William Moulton Marston, THE FAMILY CIRCLE psychologist, explained it. "This episode in American spoofology is attributable almost entirely to the comics," he told me. "Comic-strip stories like Buck Rogers,' appearing in daily newspapers and Sunday comics sections, and recently in monthly comics magazines, have created a world of fantasy that is almost as real to adults as it is to children. And that means that sane grownups sometimes cannot tell the difference between fact and fancy. There are millions of normal men and women today who have no mental resistance at all to tales of the weirdly impossible. No supernatural being is too illogical to believe in. Orson Welles' fascinating radio experiment proved that Americans today are living an imaginary mental life in a comics-created world!"

I know from observation in my own household that children read the so-called funnies morning, noon, and — unfortunately — night, and that while they're doing it there are no childish quarrels. Naturally, I had come to enjoy those peaceful interludes that followed the purchase of the magazines, but then Dr. Marston's statement made me begin to wonder if comics magazines were poisonous mental

pacifiers, and I counted how many I personally had been buying. I found that the number was constantly increasing. Other parents made the same check, and among us we counted 84 different comics magazines. And the more enterprising youngsters traded them among themselves so that they might read all of them.

Parent-teacher groups, women's clubs, and other parents' organizations were starting to be a little worried over the possible harm such assiduous comics reading might do our future generations, when Stirling North, in *The Chicago Daily News,* added to the foment with his scathing indictment of the comics magazines. North pulled no punches when he said, "The lurid publications depend for their appeal upon mayhem, murder, torture, abduction, superman heroics, voluptuous females, blazing machine guns, and hooded justice." He added that parents and teachers throughout America would be forced to band together to break the hold of the comics.

With terrible visions of Hitlerian justice in mind, I went to Dr. Marston, whose common-

"The Gumps" was the first important strip tease. It marked the comics' departure from humor and piqued curiosity by never revealing quite all

sense and farseeing views usually quiet the tempest in the teapot.

"Do you know anything about comics magazines?" I asked. "Do you know how many are sold each month?"

If I thought the question might stick the Doctor, I was wrong — as usual. He said, "There are about 108 comics magazines on the newsstands. Sales figures show that between 10,000,000 and 12,000,000 magazines are sold every month. That means $1,000,000 or more are spent every month by comics fans. There are, besides, another 3,000,000 or 4,000,000 comics magazines sold quarterly. Surveys show that on the average four children read every book sold. That makes a total of somewhere between 40,000,000 and 50,000,000 juvenile readers per month. And another 12,000,000 to 16,000,000 readers every three months. The magazines sell for 10c apiece, which brings the yearly retail sales to between $14,000,000 and $15,000,000."

When I professed amazement at the Doctor's detailed knowledge of the subject, he told me that he had been doing research in

this field for more than a year—and that *he had read almost every comics magazine published during that time!* I told him that the figures were pretty big for me, but that I gathered that just about every child in America is reading these magazines.

"That's correct," Dr. Marston said. "And surveys show that 86% of the parents enjoy reading them also. Which is still more amazing. Nothing like the comics-magazine movement has ever been known before. The comics sections of Sunday newspapers long ago became the Sabbath-day bible of more than 10,000,000 children. But now the comics magazines have become their weekday textbooks, and believe me, no youngsters ever studied their schoolbooks as they do these new comics!"

"How do you explain their appeal?" I asked. "I always assumed that the appeal of comics to children was humor. But you never see them laugh at the funnies. The one thing they take most seriously in life is their comics-magazine reading. Why is that?"

"The comics long ago ceased to be humorous," Dr. Marston said. "More than 30 years ago Bud Fisher (Harry Conway) originated the comic strip that is now the oldest one published—'Mutt and Jeff.' That was intended to be funny and thousands of readers laughed with Bud. A few years later, in 1917, along came R. Sidney Smith with a serious story continuity and grotesque characters — 'The Gumps.' You may think Andy Gump is a character to be laughed at, but Sidney Smith thought him an important human document. Even the humorous hangover which persisted in the laughable aspects of the chinless Andy was soon wiped out by such cartoon strips as 'Orphan

Popeye might be considered the forerunner of Superman in that he was one of the earliest characters to perform feats of strength that, although preposterous, captured the imagination of youngsters

Annie' and the avalanche of newspaper picture-stories which flourished during the 20 years following Andy Gump's debut. Less than half a dozen of the whole lot were ever intended to be funny. And one of those—featuring Popeye—gained national popularity and made its creator Segar rich; not because readers laugh at it, but because Popeye eats spinach and from that previously despised vegetable draws colossal strength to perform feats that provoke admiration. As scores of newspaper story-strip characters devoted themselves to adventure with increasing se-

film starring Lon Chaney. Its scenario reminded him, he said, of sorority baby parties. Citing scenes in which the title character is bound and whipped, while the female lead appears "dressed only in a chemise, with her hands tied behind her," Marston concluded that such scenes caused "a strong, disguised captivation emotion in the minds of the audience. Without a doubt, this accounts for the remarkable popularity of *The Hunchback of Notre Dame*." It's interesting to speculate that Marston's recommendations may have encouraged Universal to become the leading producer of horror films in the following decades, the purveyor of such captivating spectacles as *Frankenstein* (1931), *The Murders in the Rue Morgue* (1932), and *The Wolf Man* (1941).

Marston's unusual activities were partly the result of his exuberant personality; if he were alive today, he would probably have a radio call-in show. In his time, however, such flamboyance was viewed with suspicion by the academic establishment, and as the economic depression of the 1930s deepened, Marston's opportunities as an educator began to dry up. He had taught at Radcliffe, Tufts, Columbia, New York University, and the University of Southern California, but had never stuck down roots and established tenure. "I don't know what happened about the various teaching positions," said his son Byrne, "but I do remember when I was really small we were living up in Massachusetts with my grandmother because there just wasn't any money. He wasn't making any income. This was probably 1936 or so."

# THE ALL AMERICAN BOYS

M. C. Gaines has been credited with creating the modern comic book in 1933, when he realized the color newspaper pages produced by his employer Eastern Color Printing could be folded to produce magazines. He promoted these as giveaways, then tried newsstand sales. Later, working for the McClure newspaper syndicate, he passed on the first Superman strips to DC Comics, where the feature made the fortunes of publishers Harry Donenfeld and Jack Liebowitz. "We had four magazines at the time, and Donenfeld thought that was enough," explained Liebowitz, "so I got together with Charlie Gaines and we started our own company. That was All American." Their first offering, appropriately enough, was entitled *All-American Comics* (April 1939). Like Gaines's earlier efforts, it reprinted newspaper strips, including his favorite "Mutt and Jeff," but there was also new material like "Scribbly" by editor-artist Sheldon Mayer. This concerned a kid who was an aspiring cartoonist, and Mayer used to claim it had introduced the first super heroine when a plump housewife dressed up in long underwear and put a saucepan on her head. This practical joker was called the Red Tornado.

All American also introduced some more serious super heroes. Both the Flash and Hawkman took off in the first issue of *Flash Comics,* and Green Lantern got his start in *All-American Comics* #16 (July 1940). All three of them and more were members of the Justice Society of America in *All Star Comics,* but the company never had a bigger success than Wonder Woman. All American was merged with DC when Gaines sold out his interest in 1944. He went on to found EC Comics, which his son William made famous with innovative titles like *Tales from the Crypt* and *MAD.*

Marston continued to write during the decade, and produced his most serious academic work, *Integrative Psychology: A Study of Unit Response,* in 1931. A heavy text of 558 pages, with emphasis on physiological reactions, it was a collaboration with C. Daly King and Elizabeth Marston, but if this book was intended to shore up his standing as an educator, it does not seem to have had the desired effect. He wrote a historical novel called *Venus with Us* in 1932; *The Lie Detector Test* (1938); and several self-help tomes, including *You Can Be Popular* (1936), *Try Living* (1937), and *March On* (1941). His last book, *F. F. Proctor: Vaudeville Pioneer* (1943), confirmed his interest in show business. He also wrote numerous magazine articles, some reprinted in *Reader's Digest,* with titles like "Obey That Impulse" or "Who Influences the President More . . .

His Wife or His Mother?" He even arranged to appear, along with a lie detector, in a print ad extolling the virtues of Gillette razor blades.

Marston was using psychology as his subject matter, but also appeared to be using his psychological skills in attempts to stir up interest in himself as a commodity. Still, said Byrne Marston, "the times weren't too good," and the family counted on Elizabeth Marston's job with Metropolitan Life Insurance. "I do feel strongly," she wrote years later, "that every woman should have the experience of earning money and have the knowledge that she can support herself if she wants to." She listed her work experience as "research writing (competent hack variety), editing (14th edition of *Encyclopaedia Britannica,* sundry magazines), advertising, employee relations and such," yet

# THOSE AMAZIN' AMAZONS

Although they are depicted in Wonder Woman stories as both high-minded and peace loving, the Amazons in ancient legend and literature were another matter. In Greek their name meant "breastless," after their fabled practice of removing their right breasts to facilitate the use of bows and arrows, but generations of female archers have shown that such sacrifices are unnecessary, and might have been invented to show that these women warriors detested their own femininity. They lived without men except for mating, and killed any male offspring. In short, they were said to be a band of self-mutilating child murderers who launched violent, ultimately suicidal attacks on the social order. As feminist historian Abby Wettan Kleinbaum said, "The Amazon is a dream that men created," the equivalent of what debaters call "a straw man," an imaginary opponent set up to prove one's own prowess. In every old tale the Amazons were defeated, and the point was that women should know their place.

In one often repeated story, the Amazons fought briefly in the Trojan War, led by Penthesilea, their queen. The Greek warrior Achilles plunged his spear into her, and then was smitten by her beauty as she lay dying. The apparent lesson—that women were more likely to overcome men through erotic enslavement than through violence—was not too different from William Moulton Marston's own message. In the tale that Marston adapted for the origin of Wonder Woman, Hercules did indeed steal an Amazon queen's girdle (more of a belt, really, and possibly a symbol of her chastity), but when the Amazons retaliated with an attack on Athens they were wiped out to a woman. Marston used divine intervention to give them a happier ending, and modern feminists who view Amazons as an ideal may well owe more to comic books than to ancient myths.

These cartoons by Harry Peter accompanied
Marston's article about comics and Wonder Woman in
the Winter 1943–1944 issue of *The American
Scholar,* the journal of Phi Beta Kappa.

perhaps because she was so capable she questioned the need for a women's liberation movement in 1970. "What's all the fuss about?" she asked.

Her husband, however, had taken a more visionary view of a possible feminist movement, and he was in the newspapers again in November 11, 1937, when he gave an interview to *The New York Times* predicting that "the next one hundred years will see the beginning of an American matriarchy—a nation of Amazons in the psychological rather than physical sense," and that eventually "women would take over the rule of the country, politically and economically." It was not always clear whether any Marston statement was intended to make a point or just attract attention, but this time he was undoubtedly sincere. It's significant, however, that he saw a potential women's movement as tending toward domination rather than a bid for equality. Still, he welcomed the changes he predicted.

Marston believed women were less susceptible than men to the negative traits of aggression and acquisitiveness, and could come to control the comparatively unruly male sex by alluring them. In his book *The Art of Sound Pictures,* he advised screenwriters that "submission in love belongs to the man and not the woman," and that "her body and personality offer men greater pleasure than he could obtain in any other experience. He therefore yields to this attraction and control voluntarily, and seeks to be thus captivated." In *March On,* he wrote that "erotic love is the emotional source of that all-important social trait, willing submission to other people." In short, he was convinced that as political and economic equality became a reality, women could and would use sexual enslavement to achieve domination over men, who would happily submit to their loving authority. This was perhaps the most good-natured and optimistic solution ever offered to end the battle of the sexes, but it nonetheless failed to address the vital issue of allocating amatory assets. In any case, it's clear that Wonder Woman was inspired by Marston's utopian philosophy, which seems simultaneously daring and touchingly naïve (he doesn't seem to have imagined that power might corrupt women, or that

T H E   " L U R E "

sexually satisfied men might still cause trouble).

The most concrete result of Marston's forecast of a matriarchy was, apparently, another job: he was offered the post of consulting psychologist for *The Family Circle,* a popular women's magazine. And it was this position that led indirectly to the creation of Wonder Woman. Marston used his new forum to discuss a variety of issues, and may well have been employing his usual strategy of making statements that could provide him with further career opportunities. In the issue dated October 25, 1940, he held forth on the comic book, a recent publishing phenomenon that was under attack in some quarters. The article, called "Don't Laugh at the Comics," was credited to Olive Richard, apparently a staff writer, who interviewed Marston on topics of current interest. She sought reassurance about her children's reading matter from Dr. Marston, "whose common sense and farseeing views usually quiet the tempest in the teapot."

Marston may have startled the *Family Circle* audience by rattling off a series of statistics. "There are about 108 comics magazines on the newsstands. Sales figures show that between 10,000,000 and 12,000,000 magazines are sold every month," he said. "That makes a total of somewhere between 40,000,000 and 50,000,000 juvenile readers per month." And, he added, "86% of the parents enjoy reading them also." He claimed to have perused almost every comic book published during the last year, which suggests that Olive Richard's queries had not come out of the blue. Marston gave readers a brief history of early newspaper strips like Bud Fisher's "Mutt and Jeff," then announced that with the appearance of Jerry Siegel and Joe Shuster's Superman, "comics evolution took another huge jump ahead." Calling Superman the "ultimate embodiment of all childhood dreams of strength and power," Marston also paid tribute to M. C. Gaines, the executive who had recommended the Superman feature

23

Harry Peter's dramatic allegorical drawing appeared
in *Judge* magazine, circa 1912.

# REVUE OF THE FAMILY

MA

DAUGHTER    AND    SON-IN-LAW

IN COLLEGE    SON    AND OUT

PA

to DC Comics, and had subsequently become a partner in its sister company, All American Comics. According to Marston, Gaines possessed "the insight into fundamental emotional appeals which other publishers had lacked."

Marston also discussed the issue of violence in comics, and deplored the occasional gruesome scenes in Chester Gould's "Dick Tracy" (actually a newspaper strip). As an alternative, Marston offered a suggestion. "When a lovely heroine is bound to the stake, comics followers are sure that rescue will arrive in the nick of time," he said. "A bound or chained person does not suffer even embarrassment in the comics, and the reader, therefore, is not being taught to enjoy suffering." Marston's offering of flattery and restraint was evidently too much for M. C. Gaines to resist, and Dr. William Moulton Marston soon had a new position on the

Editorial Advisory Board of the DC and All American lines. This was not merely window dressing, since DC had already determined that its characters like Superman and Batman should neither kill their enemies nor employ firearms, and their publications would contain comics features promoting good citizenship. Marston, however, may have had more in mind.

Evidence of Marston's mastery of manipulation may be found in the memories of Sheldon Mayer, an assistant to M. C. Gaines and according to some accounts the real discoverer of Superman. He was an editor at All American Comics, and as he recalled things decades later, "there was a nasty article about comics in a parents-type magazine, written by a guy named William Moulton Marston, that Gaines took exception to. He was cynical enough and wise enough to suspect that

Niagara Falls   Sky Scrapers   California   Yellowstone Park   Florida

SEEING MISS AMERICA FIRST ...

this kind of article would cease if William Moulton Marston was contacted and persuaded to write for comics, which is exactly what happened." In short, Marston, whose article wasn't really negative, had flattered Gaines into giving him a job as a comic book expert. It was only a matter of time before Marston would create his own comic book series.

This was the type of opportunity Marston had apparently been seeking for years. The film industry might have been too big and too entrenched for him to find room at the top, but the fledgling comic book business was something else. Here was Marston's chance to combine his theories and his philosophy and his fantasies in a popular format that might conceivably find an audience of millions. He never seems to have doubted that he would succeed.

Unfortunately the exact process by which Marston created Wonder Woman remains cloaked in mystery. The broad outlines are clear, but details are elusive. At the age of ninety-nine, shortly before her death, his widow, Elizabeth Marston, said she had suggested that he create a female super hero, although none of Marston's earlier statements confirm this. "Bill studied the Greek and Latin myths in high school. With that as background, you can see that it was part of his mentality, so to speak," she said. "He used the mythological business of the Amazon," said Sheldon Mayer, but "he took some liberties with it."

Marston described the general outlines of his creative process in a letter written to the pioneering comics historian Coulton Waugh: "Among other recommendations which I made for better comics continuities was a suggestion that America's woman of tomorrow should be made the hero of a new type of comic strip. By this I meant a character with all the allure of an attractive woman but with the strength also of a powerful man. The publishers insisted that woman leads in comics had always been flops. But Mr. Gaines, who discovered Superman, offered to publish the proposed Woman strip in a comics magazine for six months if I would write it. This I agreed to do under the pen name, Charles Moulton" (the pseudonym combined the middle names of Maxwell Charles Gaines and William Moulton Marston).

Marston continued:

Frankly, Wonder Woman is psychological propaganda for the new type of woman who should, I believe, rule the world. There isn't love enough in the male organism to run this planet peacefully. Woman's body contains twice as many love generating organs and endocrine mechanisms as the male. What woman lacks is the dominance or self assertive power to put

Shortly before he started working on Wonder Woman, Harry G. Peter drew the superpowered Invisible Scarlet O'Neil for *Famous Funnies* #87 (October 1941).

over and enforce her love desires. I have given Wonder Woman this dominant force but have kept her loving, tender, maternal and feminine in every other way. Her bracelets, with which she repels bullets and other murderous weapons, represent the Amazon Princess' submission to Aphrodite, Goddess of Love and Beauty. Her magic lasso, which compels anyone bound by it to obey Wonder Woman and which was given to her by Aphrodite herself, represents woman's love charm and allure by which she compels men and women to do her bidding.

On February 23, 1941, Marston submitted his first script for what he then called "Suprema, the Wonder Woman." Nobody knows who wisely changed her name, but in his accompanying letter to Sheldon Mayer, Marston did ask to be consulted regarding any alterations "in the story, names, costumes or subject matter," so he must have approved. He acknowledged his unfamiliarity with the comics medium by letting Mayer decide about "arrangement of panels, etc.," and his lack of experience may explain why the first Wonder Woman story, when it finally appeared, contained two pages of typeset prose. Yet about some things Marston would brook no opposition. He told Mayer that "I fully

believe that I am hitting a great movement now underway—the growth in the power of women, and I want you to let that theme alone—or drop the project." Very few comic book creators could adopt that sort of tone with their editors, but Marston had apparently buffaloed everyone into believing he was financially secure and would have to be courted. As Mayer saw it, "Here we had a guy who had an entirely different kind of monetary relationship on the thing because he was a pro from another field, so he was paid like an author."

Marston selected and paid the man who drew Wonder Woman, whom he described as "Harry Peter, an old-time cartoonist who began with Bud Fisher on the *San Francisco Chronicle* and who knows what life is all about." Peter's claim to have worked on "Mutt and Jeff," one of the first important newspaper strips, may have helped him get his new job, since Marston had already written praising "Mutt and Jeff," while M. C. Gaines was such a big fan that he was reprinting Fisher's seminal strip in his flagship title *All-American Comics*. Outside of this fortuitous connection, what impressed Marston most, according to his wife, Elizabeth, was Peter's quality of "simplicity."

"Harry seemed like quite an elderly gentleman to me when he first began to do the thing," said Sheldon Mayer. "I was

Everett E. Hibbard's cover for *All Star Comics* #8 promotes two new members of the Justice Society, but doesn't mention the pages added to this issue to introduce a character called Wonder Woman.

under thirty and he was over sixty." Peter's birth date is not known, but if he did work with Fisher at the *Chronicle,* it would have been more than thirty years before he started drawing Wonder Woman in 1941. During the first decades of the twentieth century Peter's cartoons appeared in humor magazines like *Judge,* and often featured elaborate and detailed line work. His subjects were the upper classes of the bygone days before World War I, and his society girls sometimes showed the influence of the popular and prolific Charles Dana Gibson, whose famous pictures of the Gibson Girl apparently made an impression on Wonder Woman's profile. Rooted in nineteenth-century styles, Peter's work can appear stiff and quaint, yet not entirely inappropriate for the storybook world in which Marston disguised his tales of gender con-

flict and sexual liberation. And in 1941 Peter was at least a professional, while most of his competitors were young amateurs still learning their trade. Until they caught up, he was one of the best in the business.

"The selection of Harry Peter was not my idea. It was one of the compromises I made," said Sheldon Mayer. "There were a lot of things Peter did that almost verged on the grotesque. We would work on it, and after a while it started to grow on us. He began to catch on to what Marston wanted but at the same time to make the compromises that I wanted. He was the one thing that brought Marston and me together, and he was the center between us. He had no real understanding of storytelling, but he had a great skill at creating the effect that the script demanded."

Wonder Woman made her debut in

Above: The long arm of coincidence brings together Princess Diana and Diana Prince, encouraging Wonder Woman to buy another woman's identity in *Sensation Comics* #1 (January 1942).

Right: A storybook style of narrative was combined with comics to provide the background for Marston's Amazons in *All Star Comics* #8 (December 1941–January 1942). Art by Harry Peter.

…BUT MOTHER — I DON'T …NDERSTAND — I MUST SEE HIM! …I MUST KNOW WHO HE IS, HOW …HE GOT HERE! AND WHY HE …UST LEAVE? I—I LOVE HIM!

I WAS AFRAID, DAUGHTER, THAT THE TIME WOULD SOME DAY ARRIVE THAT I WOULD HAVE TO SATISFY YOUR CURIOSITY. COME — I WILL TELL YOU EVERYTHING!

## AND THIS IS THE STARTLING STORY UNFOLDED BY HIPPOLYTE, QUEEN OF THE AMAZONS, TO THE PRINCESS, HER DAUGHTER!

…n the days of Ancient Greece, …ny centuries ago, we Amazons …re the foremost nation in the …rld. In Amazonia, women ruled …d all was well. Then one day, …rcules, the strongest man in …e world, stung by taunts that …couldn't conquer the Amazon …men, selected his strongest and …rcest warriors and landed on …r shores. I challenged him to …rsonal combat—because I knew …t with my MAGIC GIRDLE, …en me by Aphrodite, Goddess …Love. I could not lose.

And win I did! But Hercules, by deceit and trickery, managed to secure my MAGIC GIRDLE— and soon we Amazons were taken into slavery. And Aphrodite, angry at me for having succumbed to the wiles of men, would do naught to help us!

With the MAGIC GIRDLE in my possession, it didn't take us long to overcome our masters, the MEN—and taking from them their entire fleet, we set sail for another shore, for it was Aphrodite's condition that we leave the man-made world and establish a new world of our own! Aphrodite also decreed that we must always wear these bracelets fashioned by our captors, as a reminder that we must always keep aloof from men.

Finally our submission to men became unbearable—we could stand it no longer—and I appealed to the Goddess Aphrodite again. This time not in vain, for she relented and with her help, I secured the MAGIC GIRDLE from Hercules.

ON---ON SPEEDS THE PLANE UNTIL IT REACHES ITS DESTINATION——WASHINGTON, D.C.!

AT LAST I'M HERE — IN THE CAPITAL OF THE UNITED STATES!

issue #8 of All American's *All Star Comics* (December 1941–January 1942). Inaugurated in the days when a comic book would often feature separate short stories about several different characters, *All Star Comics* had recently introduced the Justice Society of America, a club whose members were super heroes appearing in various All American and DC Comics. Wonder Woman would soon be involved in the Justice Society's antics, but her initial appearance was an isolated story in the back of the book, presumably placed there to stir up interest in her imminent solo series. For all its vaunted feminism, her first adventure is also a piece of flag-waving propaganda, perfectly timed to coincide with the attack on Pearl Harbor that brought Americans into World War II. The story concerns Captain Steve Trevor, an American airman who is pursu-

ing spies when his plane crashes on remote Paradise Island. All its inhabitants are women, immortal and eternally youthful, and their beautiful princess Diana nurses Trevor back to health. Her mother, Queen Hippolyte, concerned about this male intrusion, consults the goddesses Athena and Aphrodite (the Greek name for Venus) and is told to send Trevor back home, together with an Amazon champion to fight for "America, the last citadel of democracy, and of equal rights for women." An Amazon Olympics is arranged, and a disguised Princess Diana emerges victorious. Her mollified mom hands over a red, white, and blue costume "designed to be used by the winner," and Diana is suitably impressed ("Why mother, it's lovely!"). She's on her way to the U.S.A., where she will soon acquire the alter ego of hospital nurse Diana Prince.

One of Wonder Woman's more improbable accessories, her invisible plane, is introduced ferrying Steve Trevor home in *Sensation Comics* #1. Script: William Moulton Marston. Art: Harry Peter.

That's about it, except for the prose exposition in which Marston depicts Hercules as a villain who picked on the poor Amazons until Aphrodite whisked them away to Paradise Island. There they were free from the violence of men, but had to wear bracelets made of the metal Amazonium to remind them of the chains that had bound their wrists together. This emblematic jewelry also played a part in Diana's final athletic triumph. In the crowd-pleasing game of "Bullets and Bracelets," two women fire pistols at each other and try to deflect the shots with their Amazonium adornments until finally one of them is hit. In this case it was Diana's friend Mala, who ended up with a slug in her shoulder and blood streaming down her arm. Presumably she could have been killed, and this was only the first of many incidents that would belie a claim, made by Marston and others, that Wonder Woman would not resort to violence.

There is one more tale to be told about the bracelets, and it could be the most significant of all. Comics fans may not have noticed, but Marston told at least part of the truth about where Wonder Woman's decorative death-deflectors originated. In the August 14, 1942, issue of *The Family Circle,* which appeared eight months after Wonder Woman hit the newsstands, Marston was interviewed as usual by Olive Richard. Less usual by far was the way he addressed her as "my Wonder Woman!" Amid his discussions of the way women's work in World War II would help liberate them and set the stage for their ultimate ascension, Marston took time to announce that Olive Richard's

bracelets were "the original inspiration for Wonder Woman's Amazon chain bands," which "protect her against bullets in the wicked world of men." This was interesting enough in itself, but there were hints of something else in Richard's affectionately condescending references to Marston's girth and garrulousness. There was more going on here than met the eye, and the truth is that Olive Richard, like Wonder Woman, had a secret identity.

Olive Richard had originally been Olive Byrne, the student who had helped Marston with his study of the sorority "baby party" at Tufts. She is also visible, a dark-haired woman monitoring blood pressure tests, in photos of Marston's well-publicized demonstrations of the lie detector. Clearly she was collaborating with him on the *Family Circle* articles, and the suggestion that she was merely a magazine staffer asking him innocent questions was another subterfuge.

Their son Byrne Marston explained the rest of the story. "Bill Marston married Elizabeth Holloway. Then in the late 1920s Olive Richard, whose name was Olive Byrne at that time, was a student at Tufts when he was teaching there. He met her and she became friends with him later on. And they pretty much lived together, the three of them, from then on—there may have been a hiatus, but almost always. Then the children came. Elizabeth and Bill Marston had two children, my older brother Pete and my sister Olive Ann. Olive Richard had two children, one was myself and the other was my brother Donald. As far as any of us really know, Olive Byrne was never married because 'Richard' was a pseudonym she used. But

# Introducing Wonder Woman

TRADE MARK APPLICATION PENDING

"AT LAST, IN A WORLD TORN BY THE HATREDS AND WARS OF MEN, APPEARS A WOMAN TO WHOM THE PROBLEMS AND FEATS OF MEN ARE MERE CHILD'S PLAY—A WOMAN WHOSE IDENTITY IS KNOWN TO NONE, BUT WHOSE SENSATIONAL FEATS ARE OUTSTANDING IN A FAST-MOVING WORLD! WITH A HUNDRED TIMES THE AGILITY AND STRENGTH OF OUR BEST MALE ATHLETES AND STRONGEST WRESTLERS, SHE APPEARS AS THOUGH FROM NOWHERE TO AVENGE AN INJUSTICE OR RIGHT A WRONG! AS LOVELY AS APHRODITE—AS WISE AS ATHENA—WITH THE SPEED OF MERCURY AND THE STRENGTH OF HERCULES—SHE IS KNOWN ONLY AS WONDER WOMAN, BUT WHO SHE IS, OR WHENCE SHE CAME, NOBODY KNOWS!"

TO BEGIN THE STRANGE HISTORY OF "WONDER WOMAN," LET US GO OUT OVER THE SEA AND FOLLOW IN THE WAKE OF A PLANE, ENTIRELY OUT OF GASOLINE! AS WE WATCH, IT FLOUNDERS HELPLESSLY IN THE SKY, AND FINALLY CRASHES ON THE SHORES OF AN UNCHARTED ISLE SET IN THE MIDST OF A VAST EXPANSE OF OCEAN....

by

CHARLES MOULTON

BURSTING FROM THE SURROUNDING FOLIAGE, TWO BEAUTIFUL FIGURES RACE TOWARD THE WRECKED PLANE...

LOOK, PRINCESS, A STRANGE PLANE!

WELL, WHAT ARE WE WAITING FOR? COME ON, LET'S SEE IF ANYONE IS HURT!

PRINCESS, IT'S—IT'S—

A MAN! A MAN ON PARADISE ISLAND! QUICK! LET'S GET HIM TO THE HOSPITAL.

we were the biological children of Bill Marston. It was an arrangement where they lived together fairly harmoniously. Each woman had two children, and my brother and I were formally adopted by Elizabeth and Bill somewhere along the line." (According to *Who's Who*, there was another child, Fredericka, who died young, and Donald's name is given as Donn Richard.)

These living arrangements, unusual now and extraordinary in Marston's day, may have accounted for some of his career changes. Few colleges would have countenanced a professor who was living with two women and having children with both of them, so Marston may have sacrificed his academic opportunities out of affection for these two women, who apparently were friendly enough to name their kids after one another. As Marston's editor became aware of the situation, he was nonplussed but ultimately won over. "I couldn't handle the things he could handle," said Sheldon Mayer. "He had a family relationship with a lot of women, yet it was male-dominated." As Mayer described the household in Rye, New York, "Betty Marston was the mother, Dotsie Richard was the secretary, there were other people who needed homes and got them, and they all operated beautifully." Mayer ultimately became a close friend of all concerned and described Marston as "the most remarkable host, with a lovely bunch of kids from different wives and all living together like one big family—everybody very happy and all good, decent people."

One more note must be added: If Elizabeth Marston claimed in later life to

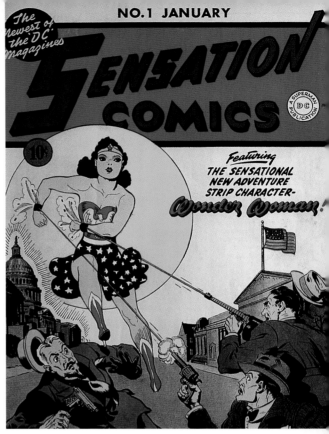

have suggested the idea of a female super hero, Byrne Marston believes that his mother, Olive "Dotsie" Richard, may have been the inspiration for Wonder Woman, and that Harry Peter may have fashioned Princess Diana to look like her. "I think physically she resembled Wonder Woman more than did Elizabeth, who was short, and nice, but not that type of woman at all." Olive Richard, on the other hand, "had black hair and blue eyes. And she was slender. And she had those big silver Indian bracelets and they were heavy. She had one on each wrist and she wore them for many, many years."

After Wonder Woman's preview appearance in the back pages of *All Star Comics,* the character was well and truly launched when she was given the lead story and the cover spot in the first issue of her new showcase *Sensation Comics* (January 1942).

33

Left: Wonder Woman's introduction in *All Star Comics* #8. Script: William Moulton Marston. Art: Harry Peter.

Above: Harry G. Peter used a pose from Wonder Woman's first story to create the patriotic cover for the publication that introduced her regular appearances: *Sensation Comics* #1 (January 1942).

THE COMMAND... AND THE GIRL FIRES POINT-BLANK AT NUMBER 7, THE MASKED MAIDEN!

THE ULTIMATE TEST OF SPEED OF EYE AND MOVEMENT! NO.7'S BRACELETS BECOME SILVER FLASHES OF STREAKING LIGHT AS THEY PARRY THE DEATH-THRUSTS OF THE HURTLING BULLETS!

"Marston had a genius for doing precisely what he said he was going to do," observed his editor Sheldon Mayer, "and that was to create a comic book that would capture an enormous readership and also have a socially conscious effect." The precise effect Marston had in mind can only be a subject for speculation, but today's feminists may have somewhat misinterpreted the situation by suggesting that Wonder Woman was intended exclusively as a role model who would encourage self-confidence in girls. Certainly that aspect was important to Marston, but Mayer felt that Marston "was writing a feminist book but not for women. He was dealing with a male audience." It's an open secret, however infrequently acknowledged, that Wonder Woman's readers have always been predominantly male (estimates run as high as 90 percent).

Then again, Marston always felt that males were the ones who needed his message most. If he really did succeed in altering the social climate, it might have been by exposing millions of boys (who would become men by the 1960s) to the ideals of feminism. After all, it's not much of a surprise that women might want to assert themselves, but it's quite a different matter when many of their supposed oppressors agree to go along with the idea.

One way Wonder Woman won male readers to her side was to wave the flag as World War II raged on. Many super heroes won their stripes fighting this good fight, but most of them, like Superman and Batman, only occasionally made it the subject of their stories. Wonder Woman couldn't leave it alone, however, especially after she gave up Diana Prince's

Putting aside pacifism in favor of patriotism, Princess Diana leads a cavalry charge on a Nazi machine-gun nest on Harry Peter's cover for *Wonder Woman* #1 (Summer 1942).

A disguised Princess Diana trades hot lead with her friend Mala in the game of "Bullets and Bracelets," reprised in the revised origin story appearing in *Wonder Woman* #1 (Summer 1942).

nursing career and got her alter ego a secretarial job with Army Intelligence in *Sensation Comics* #3 (March 1942). This kept her close to Steve Trevor, and also in on the action as far as spies and saboteurs were concerned. Her battle cry became the well-known wartime slogan "Keep 'em flying!" and in 1943 she was even shown leading marines into battle against Japanese troops.

Wonder Woman's first costumed villain, introduced in *Sensation Comics* #2 (February 1942), was Dr. Poison, a masked enemy agent whose formula "reverso" befuddled American soldiers so that they disobeyed their orders. Meanwhile military secrets were extracted with truth serum, reflecting Marston's continuing preoccupation with detecting deception. When exposed, Dr. Poison turned out to be a beautiful woman, the Japanese Princess Maru, and the gender switch marked an ideological confusion that Marston was ultimately unwilling or unable to control. It seems that Wonder Woman's foes should have been male (and certainly many were), yet a surprising number of her most interesting and energetic opponents were female. Some of Wonder Woman's comments indicate that men were just too feeble to be worthy antagonists. Marston was apparently intrigued by the dramatic possibility of depicting Princess Diana battling various vivacious vixens (they were

invariably gorgeous), or perhaps he had calculated that such encounters would be most appealing to male readers. Dr. Poison, incidentally, was only the first of several enemies to adopt masculine attire before being revealed as female.

The strangest sidekick in comics, Etta Candy enjoys her two favorite pastimes in *Sensation Comics* #4 (April 1942). Script: William Moulton Marston. Art: Harry Peter.

dent at Holliday College, where Wonder Woman asked her to distract Dr. Poison's troops by recruiting "one hundred beautiful, athletic girls." This glamorous army, usually clad in red shorts and white sweaters, would accompany Wonder Woman on countless adventures, but only red-headed Etta was granted a distinct personality. She was also the usual recipient of the telepathic distress calls that Wonder Woman sent out via another of her handy hero's helpers, the "mental radio." Etta's inevitable exclamation in any situation was "Woo woo!" (apparently in imitation of the once popular comedian Hugh Herbert, now all but forgotten). Addicted to sweets, and usually depicted clutching a box of bonbons, the pugnacious Etta served as president of the Beeta Lamda sorority. She was often shown lording it over her sorority sisters while sitting on a raised throne, stuffing her face as new pledges knelt before her and had their posteriors paddled. Evidently inspired by Marston's earlier studies of undergraduate recruitment rituals, Etta even presided over a "baby party" in which shapely students were obliged to dress like infants.

An even more colorful character in her own way was Baroness Paula von Gunther, the Axis agent who became the first Wonder Woman villain to appear regularly. Unusually ruthless, she was shown more than once committing cold-blooded murder, and began her career in *Sensation Comics* #4 (April 1942) by enslaving and

Of course there were virtuous women too, among them a whole race of Amazons, but Wonder Woman's most omnipresent allies were Etta Candy and the Holliday Girls, who also made their debut in *Sensation Comics* #2. Etta Candy filled a standard role, that of the super hero's comedy sidekick, and her short, rotund shape had echoes in figures like Plastic Man's Woozy Winks or Green Lantern's Doiby Dickles, yet even by their standards she was a bit bizarre. A former patient of Diana Prince's, Etta was a stu-

37

When her costume turns up missing, Wonder Woman dons this alternate version in *Sensation Comics* #13 (January 1943). Script: William Moulton Marston. Art: Harry Peter.

Gunther was sentenced by Queen Hippolyte to an indeterminate stay at a newly constructed Amazon penal colony nearby. Appointed as warden was Wonder Woman's old friend Mala, who later explained that the place was "sort of a college where we teach girls to be happy." Bound by a magical "Venus girdle" that induced docility, prisoners were indoctrinated in "submission to loving authority" until they reformed. If the exclusively female prison population learned to submit in the same way that Marston the prophet thought men eventually would, then Transformation Island must have been quite a lively place, and by 1943 Paula von Gunther was on the side of the good guys (in a transparent whitewash, it was explained that Nazis had kidnapped her daughter and forced her to misbehave). Paula stayed a convert, became Wonder Woman's trusted ally, and used her scientific talents for virtuous ends. Marston may have wanted the hardest possible case (a Nazi) to demonstrate the power of "loving authority," or he may have suspected that the war was

whipping American women in an effort to turn them into Nazi spies. Three issues later she met her end in the electric chair, but then was revived by one of her own inventions (this seemed only fair, since Wonder Woman had her own death-defying device, the Purple Ray). Later Paula was killed again, shot during a battle between her forces and a U.S. Cavalry unit led by Princess Diana, but since her baronial body fell into the ocean and was not recovered, astute readers knew she'd be back. All this was pretty violent by the standards of the series, but what finally stopped Paula wasn't a bullet; it was something called Transformation Island (originally Reform Island).

After launching an assault on Princess Diana's ancestral home, Paula von

winding down and Paula's usefulness was coming to an end anyway. Either way, she was the only significant character to be transformed by Transformation Island. Marston learned, as other comics creators

had, that effective villains could not be lightly cast aside, and he ended up subverting his philosophy in order to create strong stories. The other felonious females turned over to Mala's ministrations inevitably escaped to go on further rampages, creating the distinct impression that Transformation Island was a flop.

★　★　★

Wonder Woman, on the other hand, was a smashing success. By summer 1942, only a few months after her debut, a new *Wonder Woman* comic book was launched, making the Amazon one of only a handful of characters considered strong enough to carry an entire publication. Simultaneously, an All American news release revealed that the pseudonymous Charles Moulton was in fact "Dr. William Moulton Marston, internationally famous psychologist," and the announcement created considerable publicity. In the first of four stories he wrote for this inaugural issue, Marston expanded on his character's origin, adding the information that the childless, manless Queen Hippolyte had acquired a daughter by sculpting a statue of a little girl and inducing Aphrodite to grant it life. In an April 16, 1942, letter to Sheldon Mayer,

Radios shaped like potatoes were fed to lions who broadcast secrets, in the outrageous espionage plot of Princess Yasmini, from *Sensation Comics* #17 (May 1943). Art by Frank Godwin.

Readers got free buttons and comics for responding to this poll from *Sensation Comics* #5 (May 1942); the results enabled Marston to brag that Wonder Woman had more fans than her male colleagues.

Below: Black Canary, one of DC's most successful female crime fighters, as drawn by Carmine Infantino for *All Star Comics* #41 (June–July 1948).

Marston submitted the final version of the story, explaining that "after you phoned I tore the last of it apart" to insert some spy catching and to give Captain Steve Trevor a promotion. As Marston wrote,

> We now have the Amazon history, the Aphrodite versus Mars theme, Paradise Island, the anti-men rules, losing the birthright business, the mental radio, the Magic Lasso, the

Amazon Girls' sports, exposing Mala to Steve for future reference, the silent invisible plane, the Amazon-Aphrodite-Athena method of creating daughters for Amazons—a very necessary bit for later use, W.W. as a Wonder Child pulling up cherry trees, Steve a Major, Colonel Darnell as Chief of Intelligence and Diana Prince as W.W. in disguise. . . . This ought to launch our pal W.W. on both feet with new readers.

# SISTERHOOD IS POWERFUL

Wonder Woman's immense popularity, which came close to Superman and Batman's, inspired costumed female characters from several other publishers, but All American and DC Comics were not quick to capitalize on what might have been a trend. Most of the male heroes from these two related companies had girlfriends (and Hawkman had a working partner, Hawkgirl), but it was a rare woman who got her own series in the same stable with Princess Diana. Of the handful who did, all got to wear the glamorous gear, but none actually had super powers.

Liberty Belle, who got her start in *Boy Commandos* #1 (Winter 1942–1943), but spent most of her career in *Star Spangled Comics,* was created by writer Don Cameron and artist Chuck Winter. Her simple but classy costume consisted of jodhpurs and riding boots, and a high-collared blue shirt with a bell emblazoned on the front. She was really "Libby Lawrence, American girl athletic champion who escaped from the Nazi terror in Europe to work for the liberation of all oppressed people," and although she appeared in almost fifty stories, the end of World War II guaranteed her eventual demise. Another alumna of *Star Spangled Comics* was Merry, the Girl of a Thousand Gimmicks. She was Mary Pemberton, sister to the Star Spangled Kid, a patriotic hero devised by Superman's original writer, Jerry Siegel. Merry, a redhead with a black mask and a crimson cape, was devised by writer Otto Binder in 1948, but may have been a bit too gimmicky; she lasted only ten issues.

The closest thing to permanent success was enjoyed by the Black Canary, introduced by writer Robert Kanigher and artist Carmine Infantino in *Flash Comics* #86 (August 1947). A blond beauty with a black costume and fishnet stockings, Dinah Drake was a former crook and had a private eye for a boyfriend. Despite her past she was welcomed into the Justice Society of America, endured until 1951, then was revived in 1963 and is still in business today.

Wonder Woman #1 also included an adventure of the unreformed Paula von Gunther, containing an episode in which a little boy playing cowboy got to tie up Wonder Woman as part of his game ("Hi-Yah, cowboy! Let's see you lasso me!"). The inside front cover featured a photograph of Alice Marble, world's amateur tennis champion, and introduced her as associate editor of *Wonder Woman*. Also pictured was Olympic swimming champ Helen Wainwright Stelling, who offered a critique: "This Amazon girl is so human you can't help loving her! As a swimmer she is tops; why not have her try her hand at bowling?" A few months later, a *Sensation Comics* cover showed Wonder Woman dutifully knocking over tenpins bearing caricatures of Axis leaders. On a more serious note, Alice Marble soon inaugurated a new feature in each issue, "Wonder Women of History," which presented brief, inspirational biographies of prominent women in comic book form.

As the series progressed, Princess Diana would urge Amazons, Holliday Girls, and other women to excel, often encouraging them by her example. However, since she could jump 150 feet, for instance, her advice wasn't really realistic (although Harry Peter was occasionally obliged to show her friends equaling her feats). Some commentators have claimed, as did Marston, that Wonder Woman's abilities were the result of training and hard work, but there's no doubt that she had genuine super powers, and they would only increase as the years

passed. Perhaps more than any event that appeared in her undeniably interesting adventures, the mere existence of Wonder Woman, a female super hero, was inspiring in itself. Marston proudly noted that she was more popular than All American's male characters.

The series may have preached progress where women were concerned, but it was less laudable in its treatment of ethnic groups. Foreigners, even the ones Americans weren't at war with, were often

41

Top: Photographed by associate editor Alice Marble are writer William Moulton Marston, artist Harry Peter, editor Sheldon Mayer, and publisher M. C. Gaines. From *Wonder Woman* #2 (Fall 1942).

Above: Associate editor Alice Marble gets a good look at *Wonder Woman* #1 in a photo from *Sensation Comics* #9 (September 1942).

Right: Poor Mala must have been losing contests to Princess Diana ever since infancy, to judge from Marston's story recounting their childhood adventures in *Wonder Woman* #23 (May–June 1947).

Opposite: Perhaps Princess Diana's greatest enemy, the war god Mars symbolized everything she opposed. He kidnaps Steve Trevor in this story from *Wonder Woman* #2 (Fall 1942).

Below: In *Sensation Comics* #43 (July 1945), Etta Candy presides over a sorority "baby party" like the one that psychologist William Moulton Marston had studied twenty years earlier.

reduced to stereotypes, and African-Americans were subjected to degrading caricatures that should have been laid to rest by the 1940s. The mass media of the time were full of such images, but they are unpleasant nonetheless.

Males of the Caucasian persuasion were Marston's particular targets, however, and they found their most odious representative in the archenemy of Aphrodite, the war god Mars. Introduced in Wonder Woman's origin story under his Greek name Ares, he returned as Mars in *Wonder Woman* #2 (Fall 1942). In a weird mixture of mythology, astrology, and science fiction, he was depicted as ruler of the red planet that bears his name;

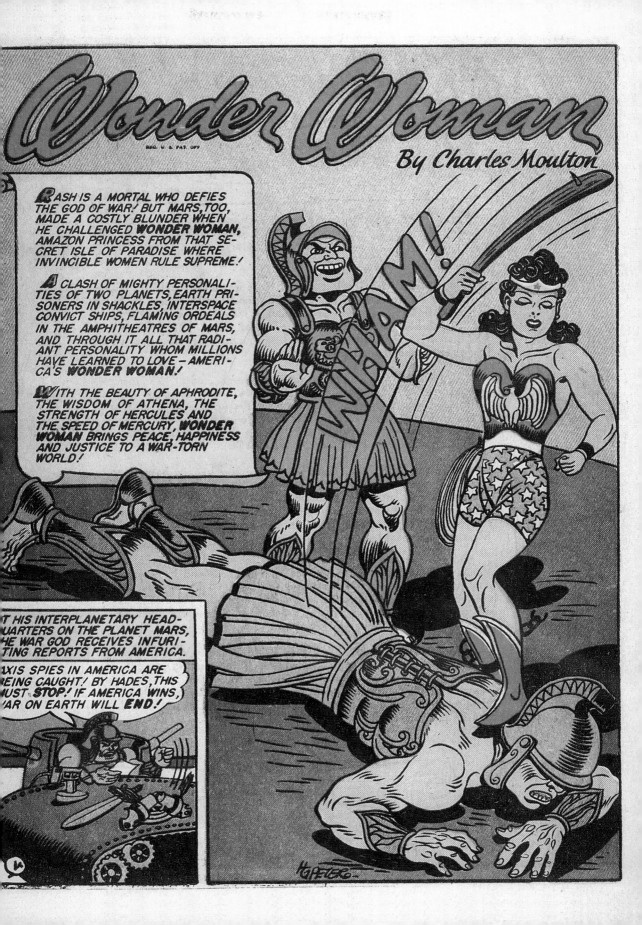

WONDER WOMAN RESTS BY THE FOUNTAIN, SIGNALING HER BIRDS TO ALIGHT IN THE TREES.

SUDDENLY, FROM THE GROUND, SPRING SINISTER FIGURES ARMED WITH DEADLY RIFLES.

WE WILL SHOOT THESE BIRDS, **WONDER WOMAN** UNLESS YOU SURRENDER YOURSELF TO US!

I-I'LL SURRENDER!

WONDER WOMAN IS CHAINED LIKE MARIE AND CARRIED AWAY.

PRISON CASTLE LOOMS AHEAD, A GRIM CREATION OF ASTRAL DOMINANCE.

BUT WITHIN THE CASTLE THE AMAZON PRINCESS IS PLACED A **THRONE**!

THIS IS CLEVER! THEY'RE TRYING TO MAKE ME **ENJOY** BEING A PRISONER BY PRETENDING TO MAKE ME A **QUEEN**!

HAIL **QUEEN**! MY FOLLOWERS BOW BEFORE YOU! ONLY CONTINUE TO WEAR CHAINS—

**CHAINS**? THESE ARE NOT CHAINS—THEY'RE MY OWN DESIRE TO REMAIN CAPTIVE—I TEAR THAT DESIRE FROM MY MIND LIKE **THIS**!

BUT THIS CASTLE WILL BE HARDER TO TEAR DOWN. IT REPRESENTS THE SPIRIT KIDNAPERS' DOMINANT DESIRE TO RULE! DOWN IT GOES!

CRUMBLE

CRASH!!

11

Wonder Woman visits a weird world on the astral plane in a tale from *Sensation Comics* #25 (January 1944), one of several suggesting Marston's interest in spiritualism.

Wonder Woman exposes the Purple Priestess as Sinestra, Nazi spy, in a scene from *Wonder Woman* #25 (September–October 1947).

although still a god, he was mortal enough for Wonder Woman to knock around, and she could be seen tossing him off a wall on the issue's cover. In a letter to his editor dated June 3, 1942, Marston referred sarcastically to "the purity of this script, the nice clean socking, blood, war, and killing," which was presumably at odds with his ultimate desire to show violence subdued by love. He also indicated that he had found a way "to work in Mr. Gaines #2's suggestion of having the big fight with Mars in the last act." The reference to "Mr. Gaines #2" indicates that script changes were being suggested by publisher M. C. Gaines's son William, who a decade later would be publishing the considerably more bloodthirsty *Tales from the Crypt*. The young Gaines made further contributions to Wonder Woman lore too, as he recalled decades later: "I created the Superman code card and also

The son of publisher M. C. Gaines helped concoct this code that only Junior Justice Society Members could crack.

the Wonder Woman code card for their clubs back in those days. One of them was a rotating disk, I believe. I came up with that idea and made a prototype."

★   ★   ★

The younger Marstons were also doing their part to keep the Wonder Woman series afloat. "We all followed it," said Marston's son Byrne. "We all got involved with it sometimes because he would give us a hundred bucks if we came up with an idea for an episode." Byrne never made much, he said, admitting that his older brother Pete "had a better imagination so he made a hundred bucks a few times."

"When I was at school at Cambridge, I used to whack out synopses and send them down to him, but it was not one hundred dollars," said Moulton "Pete" Marston. "It was a lot less than that. For just the raw ideas he used to

shoot me twenty-five or fifty dollars, which was a lot of money in those days. I did make a hundred dollars a few times, but that was for more finished work—to try to whip it into more of a script. A couple of them revolved around the character of Mars."

Byrne Marston had affectionate memories of his father: "He was a real writer. He was the kind of guy who when he had to get something done would be up all night. It was very reassuring for kids when you're little and your father is always around. You could hear him coughing because he smoked all the time. Then he would sleep half the day and be active in the evening. And in the afternoon if he got something done he would drink. He drank quite a lot, but he was a big man who could handle it fairly well."

The three Marston children who have survived all remember good times with editor Sheldon Mayer and artist Harry Peter (daughter Fredericka died at birth, and son Donn Richard, an attorney who represented Marston's estate, died at age fifty-six). "Shelly was great. We loved him," recalled Moulton Marston. "He could play musical instruments and knew more dirty stories than anyone. He used to come up and do naughty ditties for various songs, and he could relate to kids." According to Byrne Marston, "there was no generation gap, and he became a very

good friend. He would come to school and put on a little show when I was going to junior high, and he would do cartooning for the kids." Daughter Olive Ann Marston recalled Mayer as "a live wire," and said that in later years "he'd draw Scribbly and his other characters for my kids, and they were totally amazed."

For his part, Mayer explained with tongue in cheek that "what I liked about those kids was they used to love the way I played the piano, which was very bad, but it didn't matter to them because they were all tone-deaf." As for their father, Mayer acknowledged that at the office "we fought like hell, but once you went to his home you were the guest and he was the most

A page from *Wonder Woman* #15 (March 1943) encouraged her fans to fight polio (infantile paralysis) by donating dimes; their reward was an "autographed" picture of the Amazon.

AS THE AMAZON ARMY NEARS VALHALLA, THE VALKYRIES SWEEP DOWN SUDDENLY WITH A STEEL NET.

WE'VE CAUGHT THEM ALL--CLOSE THE NET!

BUT STEEL NETS MEAN NOTHING TO AMAZONS.

BAH! WHAT FRAIL METAL-- CUT YOURSELVES LOOSE, GIRLS!

PRINCESS GUNDRA, FURIOUS AT HER CAPTIVES' EASY ESCAPE, HURLS HERSELF AT THE AMAZON QUEEN.

BATTLE IS JOINED-- THE POWERFUL AMAZONS IRRESISTIBLY DRIVE BACK THE VALKYRIES.

delightful host." On at least one occasion the evening's entertainment included hooking Mayer up to a lie detector, "not because they didn't trust you but because they wanted to have fun with you." Marston "would lull you into a false sense of security," said Mayer, who then suddenly found himself confronted with the question "Do you think you're the greatest cartoonist in the world?" According to Mayer, "I felt I was being quite truthful when I said no, and it turned out I was lying! That was my first contact with the Freudian concept, and I thought the hell with that."

The Marston family was also on good terms with Harry Peter. "A great character," said Moulton, recalling "a fairly short guy, a white-haired man, because he was getting along back in those days. He always had a pipe in the corner of his mouth while he was drawing." The kids made frequent visits to the Marston Art Studio, located at Madison Avenue and Forty-third Street in New York. According to Elizabeth Marston, her husband, William, "personally handled every aspect of the production up to the point of sending to the printer. Harry Peter worked there plus several young commercial

Below right: A crime fighter turns crossing guard as Wonder Woman literally stops traffic on this amusing and inexplicably unpublished cover by Harry Peter.

One reason old comics are so rare is that kids were urged to turn them in for wartime salvage, as Wonder Woman tells her mom in *Comic Cavalcade* #6 (Spring 1944).

artists who drifted in and out. These were usually women." Byrne spent time at the studio as a boy, and remembers "young girls, like Helen Schepens, who were very attractive. It was a nice atmosphere." The assistants would handle aspects like backgrounds and lettering, but Peter "would do most of the Wonder Woman figures," according to Byrne. At one point the lettering was being done by Louise Marston, Moulton's wife.

The youngest of the children, Olive, remembers Harry Peter's kindness. "I was small. Harry was a very gentle man. He would put me on a stool and ask me to be quiet, and I could watch him draw," she said. "I was a very good kid because I was so amazed. It was very impressive." Olive

was taken to the office by another member of "this Wonder Woman network," Marjorie Wilkes. "She was one of Mom's dearest friends, and she lost her husband to the influenza, and so she came to live with us also," Olive explained. "I think that the gut work was done between Marjorie and Dad, because she was the one who helped name her Wonder Woman. She used to do a lot of the lettering, and when he wrote the scripts she would be the one to type them up. She was a good lady."

★   ★   ★

If Wonder Woman had become a cottage industry, it was almost a matter of necessity

Wonder Woman astride a bucking bronco, in a spirited drawing by Harry Peter that may have been intended as a cover idea.

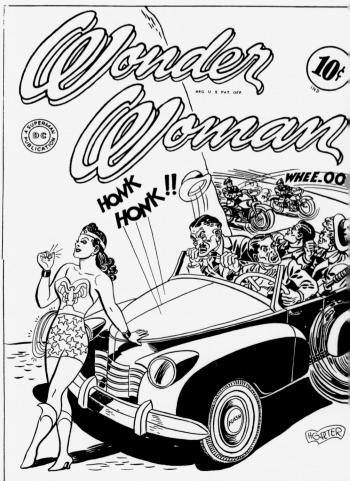

# Wonder Woman Explains Waste Paper Salvage

HELLO, DAUGHTER, I'VE BEEN WATCHING THE PEOPLE OF AMERICA THRU THE MAGIC SPHERE.. I'VE SEEN SOME STRANGE THINGS....

STRANGE THINGS, MOTHER?

YES. WOMEN SEEM TO BE USING THEIR OWN SHOPPING BAGS INSTEAD OF HAVING THEIR PURCHASES WRAPPED FOR THEM.... CHILDREN HAVE BEEN CAREFULLY SAVING OLD NEWSPAPERS AND---

WHY, MOTHER-- THAT'S NOT STRANGE--- IT'S BECAUSE OF THE WAR-

THE WAR? WHAT'S THE WAR GOT TO DO WITH SAVING PAPER? WEAPONS ARE MADE OF STEEL! LOOK AT THIS SWORD--- BEST SWORD IN THE WORLD-- BUT IT'S NOT MADE OF PAPER.!!

BUT, MOTHER--

THIS WAR AMERICA IS FIGHTING IS A NEW BIG KIND OF WAR-- AND YOU'D BE SURPRISED HOW IMPORTANT A PART PAPER PLAYS IN IT!

MAGIC SPHERE

AMERICA 1943-44

"WELL---LET'S TURN THE MAGIC SPHERE TO THE AMERICAN TROOPS IN THE BATTLE ZONE --- AND LEARN SOME OF THE USES OF PAPER---

RATIONS-- PACKED IN PAPER!

"--- CARTRIDGES AND SHELLS ARE WRAPPED IN PAPER --- THE SOLDIERS' SHOES ARE LINED WITH IT.!"

PAPER IS BEING CONVERTED INTO BOMB BANDS, PRACTICE BOMBS, WING TIPS, AIRPLANE SIGNALS, PARACHUTE FLARES---AND MANY OTHER ESSENTIALS OF WAR!"

MY GOODNESS! NOW I SEE THAT PAPER IS VERY VITAL ---THE CHILDREN OF AMERICA SHOULD SPARE NO EFFORT ---

YES, BOYS AND GIRLS---NO EFFORT IS TOO GREAT---EVERY OUNCE COUNTS --- SAVING YOUR OWN WASTE PAPER IS NOT ENOUGH! HELP COLLECT THE SALVAGE---AND PACK IT.! ASK YOUR TEACHER ABOUT ORGANIZING SALVAGE GROUPS-- YOU CAN BE OF GREAT HELP- GET BUSY.!!

# GOOD GIRLS DON'T, BUT I DO

Some commentators believed the Wonder Woman comics contained certain sexual undertones, but the artwork was a mitigating circumstance. Harry Peter's bold brush strokes turned every drawing into a cartoon, and his characters were more like abstract concepts than sensual simulations, but some of his poses would have looked more suggestive if drawn by different hands. Other comic book artists delineated their beautiful women in a way that made even innocent situations seem sexy, and modern collectors refer to this 1940s phenomenon as "good girl art." The adjective described the style rather than its subjects, who were not required to exhibit exceptional virtue.

One company specializing in this approach was Fiction House, whose most famous character was a female version of Tarzan called Sheena, Queen of the Jungle. She appeared in *Jumbo Comics*; other Fiction House titles included *Planet Comics* and *Jungle Comics.* The jungle setting was fraught with employment opportunities for wild women, and nobody exploited them better than a publisher named Victor Fox. A former DC accountant, he began his career with an imitation of Superman so blatant that it was put out of business after only one issue. By the late 1940s, Fox Features specialized in

jungle comics like *Rulah, Jungle Goddess* and *Jo-Jo, Congo King,* many containing slick artwork by the likes of Jack Kamen and Al Feldstein, and all featuring a combination of scantily clad bodies and bloody violence. The jewel in the company's crown was Phantom Lady, a costumed crime fighter picked up from Quality Comics and refashioned by the king of good girl art, Matt Baker. One of the few African-American artists working in comics, Baker had a gift for drawing bold, voluptuous beauties. His cover for *Phantom Lady #17* (April 1948) showed the title character not nearly as tied up as Wonder Woman often was, but looking so provocative that Phantom Lady became the poster child for those who insisted that comic books should be censored.

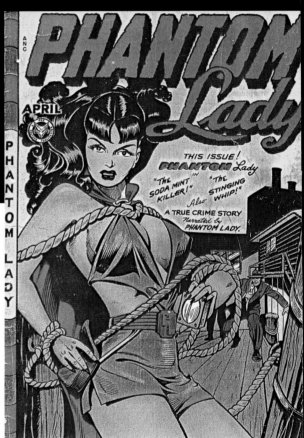

as the character became increasingly successful. She had a story in every monthly issue of *Sensation Comics*, filled entire issues of *Wonder Woman*, and when *Comic Cavalcade* #1 appeared in Winter 1942, another of her adventures was scheduled for each quarterly issue. As if this weren't enough, Marston also felt obliged to oversee the Amazon's association with the Justice Society of America, even rewriting someone else's script for *All Star Comics* when Wonder Women was seriously involved in one of the group's adventures. "We figure Wonder Woman's total magazine circulation at around two and a half million," Marston wrote.

The burden on Marston grew even heavier when, in April 1944, he and M. C. Gaines signed contracts with the King Features syndicate for a daily Wonder

Woman newspaper strip. Almost anyone else would have farmed out some of these writing chores, but there is no indication that Marston had help outside his family circle. He was firmly convinced that only he knew how to deliver his message of "psychological propaganda," and no

Turned into a collector's item by its detractors, Matt Baker's cover for *Phantom Lady* #17 (April 1948) is a classic example of what would become known as "good girl art."

Looking like a wedding present, Wonder Woman is all tied up in ribbon for *Comic Cavalcade* #8 (Fall 1944), but the blushing bride won't make it to the altar.

# WONDER WOMAN

### By CHARLES MOULTON

AT LAST, **HERE'S** THE GREAT EVENT YOU'VE BEEN WAITING FOR— **STEVE** CAPTURES **WONDER WOMAN** FOR HIS BRIDE! BUT STRANGE HAPPENINGS BESET THE JOYFUL PATH OF THE BRIDAL PAIR. EVERY CIRCUMSTANCE THAT EVER AROSE TO FORESTALL A WEDDING, PALES TO INSIGNIFICANCE COMPARED TO WHAT HAPPENED WHEN THE WEDDING MARCH PLAYED FOR **WONDER WOMAN**!

THE GIRL FROM PARADISE ISLAND, BEAUTIFUL AS APHRODITE, WISE AS ATHENA, STRONGER THAN HERCULES AND SWIFTER THAN MERCURY, FOUND HERSELF IN THE MOST PUZZLING PREDICAMENT OF HER ENTIRE CAREER WHEN SHE PROMISED TO BECOME— "THE AMAZON BRIDE."

ONE EVENING AFTER DIANA AND STEVE HAVE BEEN WORKING LATE AT THE OFFICE.

COME ON, M'GIRL, YOU'VE KEPT YOUR NOSE TO THE GRINDSTONE LONG ENOUGH—LET'S RELAX AND GO TO A NIGHT CLUB, OR SOMETHING!

OH NO, STEVE, I MUSTN'T—

**①**

doubt was eager to hold on to the maximum amount of income after years of hard times.

The newspaper strip offered new opportunities, and according to Marston, "It is my hope to make this strip as appealing to adults as it has proved to the juvenile readers of comics magazines. Wonder Woman is now running in *Gearshifters,* a serviceman's newspaper in New Caledonia, and the special services officer in charge reports that the boys there are crazy about my girl friend, the princess." On May 8, 1944, the princess made her debut in papers, including the *New York Journal-American,* but a year later she was gone. According to comic strip historian Bill Blackbeard, the strip simply wasn't picked up by enough important papers, and lacking this distribution, "it never made money." The problem may have been Wonder Woman's colleagues in the super hero business. Superman hit the newspapers in 1939 and ran continuously until 1966. When the Batman strip was introduced in 1943, many papers felt they couldn't squeeze it into their limited space without dropping the already proven Superman, and the Caped Crusader was canceled after three years. Bucking this kind of competition, Wonder Woman found an opponent she couldn't defeat, but just getting a shot at syndication showed how powerful she had become, since very few contenders from the comic books ever got into the newspapers at all.

\* \* \*

The Amazon continued to triumph in comic books, taking a setback like the loss of her daily strip in stride. Marston's creativity was at its peak in the mid-1940s, and Wonder Woman's opponents kept getting wilder. A case in point was Dr. Psycho, a diminutive misogynist who first showed up in *Wonder Woman #5* (June–July 1943). A brilliant scientist, not unreasonably annoyed to be subjected to incessant insults because he was short and ugly, Dr. Psycho was framed for robbery and became a woman hater after his fiancée Marva not only believed him guilty but married his accuser, the real thief. Upon his release Psycho murdered the usurper, and by hypnotizing Marva persuaded her to marry him. Under the influence of Mars, he developed occult powers and embarked on a campaign against women, using the enslaved Marva to produce ectoplasm that could create a duplicate of any human being.

Marston enjoyed Dr. Psycho so much that he brought back the little lunatic for another story in the same issue, getting him out of prison through the use of an ectoplasmic double who seemed to be Psycho's corpse. It was a trick Psycho would use more than once over the years, but the authorities just kept on sending him back to jail again so he could escape and commit additional outrages; he murdered Steve Trevor's secretary, and even

succeeded in imitating Wonder Woman. These stories represented just one example of Marston's interest in psychic phenomena; in other tales he showed characters engaged in astral travel, or visiting the spirit world, or manifesting thought forms on the material plane. Whether he genuinely believed in such things or simply found them to be interesting plot material is not clear.

Immediately after Dr. Psycho got his start, Marston unleashed another great villain, the Cheetah, in *Wonder Woman* #6 (Fall 1943). This was one wicked woman whose disposition couldn't be improved by trips to Transformation Island, even though before her inevitable escape she would be begging, "Keep me here in

OTHER FULL-LENGTH ADVENTURE OF THE JUSTICE SOCIETY of AMERICA—
E MYSTERY OF THE METAL MENACE!

## THE SUPER SOCIAL SECRETARY

*All Star Comics,* home to the Justice Society of America, had provided a place for the initial Wonder Woman story, and before long she was a part of the world's first club for super heroes. In *All Star Comics* #11 (June–July 1942), the issue prepared after Pearl Harbor, the Amazon appeared "as guest star in a national emergency." Not too coincidentally, this issue appeared simultaneously with the debut of her new solo comic book, which it doubtless helped to promote. Joining Hawkman, Dr. Midnite, the Atom, the Spectre, Dr. Fate, the Sandman, Johnny Thunder, and Starman, Wonder Woman starred in a segment where she slapped around Japanese soldiers invading the Philippines.

In *All Star Comics* #12 (August–September 1942), the Justice Society leader, Hawkman, announced, "Wonder Woman has volunteered to be our secretary while we are at war." Such a pedestrian position has seemed to some like evidence of sexism, but the situation was complex. The JSA was designed to provide more exposure for its members; hence heroes with their own comic books (Superman, Batman, Green Lantern, the Flash) became honorary members and ceased to appear. So Wonder Woman was getting a break with her Justice Society walk-ons, especially since she kept showing up on covers. But when regular writer Gardner Fox gave her a full segment in *All Star Comics* #13 (October–November 1942), William Moulton Marston objected and insisted on writing about her visit to Venus himself. Marston later sent her back to the planet, where women had wings to fly away from unworthy men, and would eventually envision strange civilizations throughout the entire solar system, but Fox evidently didn't relish being rewritten. Wonder Woman never got another major role until after Marston's death, when she suddenly became a full member once again.

**W**HILE WONDER WOMAN is entirely new as a daily newspaper strip, it has long enjoyed tremendous popularity with more than 10,000,000 readers of comic books.

In a recent survey made in the city of Hudson, N.Y. among 1125 families WONDER WOMAN was first of 135 comic book characters tested with girls of from 8 to 17 years and second with adult women.

Thus, WONDER WOMAN comes to you as a new and entirely different newspaper feature, but with 10,000,000 ardent fans following her daring exploits and adventures.

*King*

**FEATURES**

**SYNDICATE**

This extremely rare brochure from King Features Syndicate
promotes the short-lived Wonder Woman newspaper strip
by Marston and Peter.

**Wonder Woman** · By Charles Moulton

Page mechanicals for two weeks of strips (May 29–June 10, 1944).

Amazon prison and train me to control my evil self!" Her problem was a split personality: When she wasn't wearing the spotted Cheetah costume, she was known in high society as debutante Priscilla Rich. Insanely jealous of Wonder Woman, she snapped her cap and developed an alternate personality as "a treacherous, relentless huntress." Trapped in a fire at the end of her first appearance ("Arr-rr-rgh!"), the Cheetah bounced back to become Wonder Woman's most resilient and malicious foe. She would abuse her slave girls, indulge in espionage, and even kidnap Princess Diana's mom, but all Priscilla got

in return from the painfully patient Wonder Woman was a tip that she might be happier if she took up dancing. Slithering around in a skintight kitty costume years before Catwoman acquired hers in the Batman comics, the Cheetah may have been the most ferocious felonious feline female in the funnies.

If one wicked woman wasn't enough, Marston would whip up a whole lost city full of them, as he did in *Wonder Woman* #8 (Spring 1944). The story took place in a legendary sunken city, where an army of Amazons from Atlantis struggled for power among themselves while dominat-

ing their helpless men. Wonder Woman's battles against their tyrannical Queen Clea took up the entire issue. Marston used this long form more frequently than most of his contemporaries in the 1940s, giving these issues of Wonder Woman an epic quality. Marston appreciated a big canvas and he liked big characters too; his Atlantean Amazons were oversized, and the theme of huge and menacing beauties would resurface repeatedly in his work. A case in point was Giganta, whose introduction followed Queen Clea's and took

up all of *Wonder Woman* #9 (Summer 1944). Giganta was a female gorilla turned into a gorgeous redhead by a screwball scientist, and it's a good bet that Marston got the idea from a 1943 film produced by his old employer, Universal Pictures. It's not likely that he could have resisted taking a look at a movie called *Captive Wild Woman.*

The theme of captivity, in fact, was stirring up some controversy. A glance at almost any Wonder Woman story of the period would show numerous images of

Left: Employing his hypnotic powers, Dr. Psycho whips up a batch of ectoplasm as part of his escape plan in *Wonder Woman* #5 (June–July 1943). Script: William Moulton Marston. Art: Harry Peter.

Above: The Cheetah's split personality shows its artistic side, and Wonder Woman demonstrates her grasp of psychology, in a bizarre episode from *Sensation Comics* #22 (October 1943). Art by Harry Peter.

Right: Wonder Woman falls prey to a witch, a fox, a vulture, and a lecherous bunny rabbit in this scene from an unpublished story drawn by Harry Peter circa 1946.

women in bondage, a concept that Marston claimed cut down on violence, but which he certainly knew was sexually stimulating to some people. The Amazons used Venus Girdles and Magic Lassos to subdue their lovely prisoners, the female villains seemingly always had flocks of fettered slave girls, and once it had been revealed that Wonder Woman could lose her powers if her bracelets were chained together, every evildoer seemed willing and able to get the job done. Technically, the welding had to be done by a man to have the desired effect, but each bad gal seemed to keep a guy on the payroll for just such a purpose. Virtually every story seemed to show a helpless Princess Diana trussed up in some ingenious manner, emphasized at some point by displaying her full-length form in a large vertical panel.

Some feminists who are uncomfortable with the theme insist that there was no special emphasis on bondage in Wonder Woman's adventures, but Marston knew it was there, and so did his publisher, his editor, and his public, not to mention the other advisers who had been hired along with Marston to supervise the content of the comics. Their discussions, preserved in correspondence, constitute a fascinating casebook on the perennial controversy concerning censorship and popular culture. "There was a certain symbolism that Marston engaged in, which was very simple and very broad," said editor Sheldon Mayer. "I suspect it probably sold more comic books than I realized, but every time I came across one of those tricks, I would try to clean it up. I probably made it worse. But the fact is, it was a runaway best-seller."

Marston's most concerned in-house critic was Josette Frank of the Child Study Association of America. She was one of the experts employed to keep an eye on the comics, and in a February 17, 1943, letter to publisher M. C. Gaines, she wrote, "There has been considerable criticism in our committee concerning

63

Left: Wonder Woman regains a grip on herself with bracelets that are "tighter than ever," but not until she's wreaked havoc on a nest of Nazis. Art from *Sensation Comics* #19 (July 1943) by Frank Godwin.

your Wonder Woman feature, both in *Sensation Comics* and in the *Wonder Woman* magazine. As you know, I have never been enthusiastic about this feature. I know also that your circulation figures prove that a lot of other people *are* enthusiastic. Nevertheless, this feature does lay you open to considerable criticism from any such group as ours, partly on the basis of the woman's costume (or lack of it), and partly on the basis of sadistic bits showing women chained, tortured, etc. I wish you would consider these criticisms very seriously because they have come to me now from several sources."

Dorothy Roubicek, who would eventually become an editor of romance comics but who had just joined All

American a few months earlier, was apparently assigned by Gaines to research the situation. In her initial memo, dated February 19, 1943, she suggested that many tricky situations could be avoided if Wonder Woman simply kept away from the heated atmosphere of Paradise Island. She also considered the costuming issue and enclosed "a sketch of the type of clothes I would suggest—feminine and yet not objectionable—as those short, tight panties she wears might be." Gaines duly fired the drawing off to Marston, after scrawling a note across the page: "Doc: She did this without even knowing how close she came to the original costume!" Roubicek's design is similar to a simple Greek tunic, which might have been considered in Wonder Woman's planning stage. Or perhaps Gaines was

**65**

Above: Wonder Woman amuses herself by pretending to be her namesake, housewife Diana Prince, in *Sensation Comics* #9 (September 1942). Script: William Moulton Marston. Art: Harry Peter.

Left: Dorothy Roubicek drew this proposed new costume for Wonder Woman, a variant on the ancient Greek tunic that was designed to replace those star-spangled, skintight pants.

MEN CHAINED MY BRACELETS TOGETHER! BY APHRODITE'S DECREE, MY AMAZON STRENGTH IS GONE!

Left: For years, virtually every story showed Wonder Woman in an oversize bondage panel, like this one from *Sensation Comics* #35 (November 1944)

simply referring to her first appearance, when Wonder Woman wore a skirt, which was immediately exchanged for shorts because, in some scenes of the Amazon in action, the skirt seemed considerably less modest.

On February 20, Marston wrote a four-page letter to Gaines, intended to refute Josette Frank's charges. He began with a personal attack, calling Frank "an avowed enemy of the Wonder Woman strip, of me and also of you insofar as she predicted this strip would flop and you rubbed it into her that it hadn't." He also said she had "a determined drive to ruin this Wonder Woman strip if possible, or injure it all she can, and you can bet she's doing that everywhere she goes, despite the fact that you are paying her to work for you." Psychology is not an exact sci-

Below left: Locked in a box and bouncing bullets off her bracelets, Princess Diana is at least getting her ropes broken in this wild splash page by Peter from Sensation Comics #33 (September 1944).

Below: In *Sensation Comics* #33 (September 1944), a party where guests impersonate super heroes provides a chance for Harry Peter to draw the Flash, Superman, Batman, and the Spectre.

ence, and evidently there were bitter fights behind the benign façade of the advisory board for All American and DC Comics.

Addressing Frank's specific charges, Marston referred to the old magazine article that had first brought him to Gaines's attention. "Sadism consists in the enjoyment of other people's actual suffering," he reiterated. "Since binding and chaining are the one harmless, painless way of subjecting the heroine to menace and making drama of it, I have developed elaborate ways of having Wonder Woman and other characters confined." Indeed, said Marston, he was promoting the idea that "confinement to WW and the Amazons is just a sporting game, an actual enjoyment of being subdued. This, my dear friend, is the one truly great contribution of my

Wonder Woman strip to moral education of the young. The only hope for peace is to teach people who are full of pep and unbound force to *enjoy* being bound." He asserted, "Women are exciting for this one reason—it is the secret of women's allure—women *enjoy* submission, being bound. This I bring out in the Paradise Island sequences where the girls beg for chains and enjoy wearing them." Furthermore, he continued, "because all this is a universal truth, a fundamental subconscious feeling of normal humans, the children love it. That is why they like Wonder Woman on Paradise Island better than anywhere else." In conclusion, Marston said, "I have devoted my entire life to working out psychological principles," and insisted that he deserved "free rein on fundamentals."

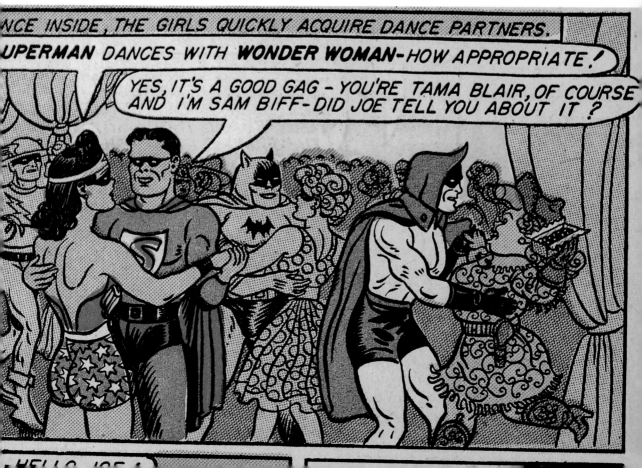

Soldiering on, Dorothy Roubicek visited another member of the board, Dr. Lauretta Bender, in her office at Bellevue Hospital in New York City. In a March 12 memo to Gaines, Roubicek encapsulated Bender's opinions:

1. She does not believe that Wonder Woman tends toward masochism or sadism.
2. She believes that Dr. Marston is handling very cleverly this whole "experiment" as she calls it.

The next voice to join the chorus belonged to W. W. D. Sones, professor of education at the University of Pittsburgh. In a March 15 letter to Gaines, Sones stated, "I have not had for a long time so interesting a problem for analysis," and called the whole business "both comic and tragic." Upon reading Wonder Woman for the first time since her inception, Sones said, "My impressions confirmed those of Miss Frank that there was a considerable amount of chains and bonds, so much so that the bondage idea seemed to dominate the story. True enough, cruelty and suffering seem not to be involved (in line with Dr. Marston's interpretation of sadism)." However, wrote Sones, "I was not impressed with Dr. Marston's argument; the social purpose which he claims is open to very serious objection. It is just such submission that he claims he wants to develop that makes dictator dominance possible. From the standpoint of social ideals, what we want in America and in the world is cooperation and not submission. Indeed, as I studied the author's letter I could not help but feel that such subtle and almost mystic purposes were a business and a social risk."

Nobody, not even Marston, denied that the Wonder Woman stories were full of bondage, but deciding what that meant might be another matter. Whether scenes were sadistic was perhaps, as Sones suggested, a matter of "interpretation." The characters trapped helplessly in the stories

A rare adventure starring Etta Candy and her class-mates, this western adventure saw the light of day in *Comic Cavalcade* #7 (Summer 1944).

were often a split second away from being burned or crushed or punctured, which Marston said wasn't torture because everyone knew they would escape. Yet people both good and bad did die in Marston's stories, which nevertheless were not very violent compared to other comic books of the era. Part of people's problems with the pictures may have stemmed from the fact that the figures in jeopardy were so often female, which in a world of gender equality actually shouldn't have made any difference.

Marston made his most elaborate defense on March 20, in reply to the letter from Sones. He admitted that his letter of February 20 "did not present my argument in a form suitable for scientific or academic discussion—in fact it was intended only for Mr. Gaines personally." Marston repeated many arguments he'd been making ever since he wrote *Emotions*

# ALL-AMERICAN COMICS, Inc.

480 LEXINGTON AVE. ★ Telephone: PLaza 3-0740 ★ NEW YORK, N. Y.

LICENSORS AND PUBLISHERS OF

**FLASH COMICS ★ ALL-AMERICAN COMICS ★ ALL-STAR COMICS
SENSATION COMICS ★ ALL-FLASH ★ WONDER WOMAN
GREEN LANTERN ★ MUTT & JEFF ★ COMIC CAVALCADE
★ Also "PICTURE STORIES FROM THE BIBLE" ★**

*Editorial Offices*
225 LAFAYETTE STREE
TELEPHONE: CAnal 6-7

September 14, 1943

Dr. William Moulton Marston
Cherry Orchard
Rye, New York

Dear Doc:

Attached is a copy of a letter which came in yesterday's mail. I'd like to discuss this with you the next time you come in.

This is one of the things I've been afraid of, (without quite being able to put my finger on it) in my discussions with you regarding Miss Frank's suggestions to eliminate chains.

Miss Roubicek hastily dashed off this morning the enclosed list of methods which can be used to keep women confined or enclosed without the use of chains. Each one of these can be varied in many ways - enabling us, as I told you in our conference last week, to cut down the use of chains by at least 50 to 75% without at all interfering with the excitement of the story or the sales of the books.

Sincerely,

M. C. Gaines, President
ALL-AMERICAN COMICS, INC.

MCG/g
Encls.

Above: Inspired by a soldier's concupiscent correspondence, this 1943 note from publisher Gaines to
creator Marston came at the peak of the bondage

Right: Tied with her own golden lasso, Wonde
Woman takes several pages to work her way free i
what may be her most extreme bondage episode

**WONDER WOMAN,** MEANWHILE, STRAINS DESPERATELY FORWARD AGAINST HER BRIDLE ROPE.

I **MUST** GET FREE AND WARN MOTHER!

THE AMAZON MAID'S POWERFUL MUSCLES PROVE TOUGHER THAN THE HICKORY TREE.

SNA-AP!

ANABLE TO LOOSEN THE UNBREAKABLE LASSO WHICH BINDS HER, WONDER WOMAN ROLLS OVER AND OVER TO AN OPEN FIELD.

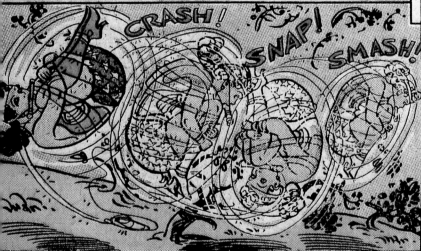

CRASH! SNAP! SMASH!

CLENCHING HER JAWS WITH GRIM DETERMINATION, THE PRINCESS CRUSHES THE WOODEN GAG BETWEEN HER TEETH.

I NEED MY MOUTH FREE, BUT NOT FOR TALKING!

WONDER WOMAN SUMMONS HER PLANE BY MENTAL RADIO.

ROBOT CONTROL, TAKE OFF - LOWER LADDER - FOLLOW MY BRAIN BROADCAST BEAM -

AS HER PLANE SWOOPS SWIFTLY DOWN, THE MIGHTY AMAZON SEIZES ITS FLYING LADDER IN HER TEETH.

*of Normal People* in 1928. "Only when the control of self by others is more pleasant than the unbound assertion of self in human relationships can we hope for a stable, peaceful human society," he wrote. "Giving to others, being controlled by them, submitting to other people cannot possibly be enjoyable without a strong erotic element—enjoyment of submission to others." He also acknowledged the concerns Sones raised about the danger of submitting to tyrants, and offered up his usual recommendation of a "beneficent mistress," also employing the term "love chains." He then raised "a minor point" and pursued it for hundreds of words in the following vein: "normal males get their maximum of love happiness from being controlled, captured, or captivated by women." In that case, wouldn't the comics have sold even better if men were the ones all tied up in knots? And why did Marston tell Gaines that women were the ones who enjoyed submitting? Could he

have been deliberately using the titillating idea of women in bondage to lure chauvinistic male readers into stories that demonstrated female superiority?

Things had become so confused that the controversy might have collapsed under its own weight if not for the intervention of the U.S. Army. On September 20, 1943, a sergeant in the 291st Infantry sent a concerned but extremely courteous letter to "Charles Moulton," Wonder Woman's imaginary creator. "I am one of those odd, perhaps unfortunate men who derive an extreme erotic pleasure from the mere thought of a beautiful girl chained or bound," he wrote. "I hope you'll forgive my apparently very poor manners, but the subject is a vital one to me, and you can always tear up your fan-mail and throw it away if you want to. Have you the same interest in bonds and fetters that I have?"

The note was received by an increasingly befuddled Gaines. "This is one of

# Wonder Woman

### By Charles Moulton

TRAGEDY SEEMED TO FOLLOW POOR EDGAR ALL THRU HIS YOUNG LIFE—HIS DAD HAD BEEN SHOT AND HIS MOTHER WAS SENT TO PRISON FOR HIS FATHER'S MURDER! EVERYBODY THOUGHT THAT WAS WHY HE WAS SUCH A DULL, LONELY KID—BUT THAT WASN'T THE **REAL** REASON, AS **WONDER WOMAN** DISCOVERED WHEN SHE UNDERTOOK A FIERCE AND HECTIC STRUGGLE AGAINST SINISTER FORCES TO GIVE EDGAR AND HIS MOTHER A NEW WORLD!
NONE BUT THE **PRINCESS FROM PARADISE**, BEAUTIFUL AS APHRODITE, WISE AS ATHENA, STRONGER THAN HERCULES AND SWIFTER THAN MERCURY COULD STRAIGHTEN OUT THE TANGLED THREADS OF AN UNHAPPY CHILD'S LIFE AND BRING HIM JOY AGAIN AS **WONDER WOMAN** DOES IN THIS STORY OF "**EDGAR'S NEW WORLD**"!

152-21 43

WONDER WOMAN AWARDING PATRIOTIC PRIZES TO SCHOOL CHILDREN AT BOURBON CITY, IS MOBBED BY YOUNG ADMIRERS.

HI, **WONDER WOMAN!**

SIGN MY BOOK, **WONDER WOMAN!**

YOUR SPEECH WAS SWELL!

GEE SHE'S **BEAUTIFUL!**

1

the things I've been afraid of (without quite being able to put my finger on it)," he told Marston. He also mentioned that Dorothy Roubicek, who was certainly earning her pay, had "hastily dashed off the enclosed list of methods which can be used to keep women confined or enclosed without the use of chains." That document, unfortunately, has not survived.

"I have the good Sergeant's letter in which he expresses his enthusiasm over chains for women—so what?" responded Marston. "Some day I'll make you a list of all the items about women that different people have been known to get passionate over," he continued. "You can't have a real woman character in any form of fiction without touching off many readers' erotic fancies. Which is swell, I say—harmless erotic fantasies are now generally recognized as good for people." Gaines, in the face of so much contradictory advice, apparently decided that things were "swell" as well, and pretty much let Marston have his way for as long as he wrote Wonder Woman.

On January 29, 1944, Josette Frank asked to have her name removed from the advisory board for *Sensation Comics* and *Wonder Woman*. "Intentionally or otherwise, the strip is full of significant sex antagonisms and perversions," she wrote. "Personally, I would consider an out-and-out strip tease less unwholesome than this kind of symbolism." She may have been hoping to have the last word, but both Marston and Dr. Lauretta Bender of Bellevue dismissed Frank's reading of the symbols as a symptom of her own personal problems.

The overworked Dorothy Roubicek

had to interview Dr. Bender again, and hear her explain that in fact "*neither Dr. Marston nor Miss Frank* realized the symbolism expressed in the strip." According to Bender, the symbols that mattered most to children were methods of transportation, especially boats, and particularly

ones flying flags. "A boat itself is practically always the child's mother," she explained. "The flag is a phallic symbol, and represents the father. The sun in the background usually represents the father also." Furthermore, "submarines usually represent a threatening or bad father, and also represent the phallic symbol. When a

Left: William Moulton Marston predicted the hole in the earth's ozone layer, then used it to introduce lovely but lethal Sun Warriors in *Sensation Comics* #71 (November 1947).

boat with an American symbol is being bombed by a Nazi airplane, it is the good mother being destroyed by the bad father." She concluded that when writers "do not realize what these planes and boats and subs mean to the children reading the strips, mistakes are sometimes made." Wading through these deep waters in her first months on the job, poor Dorothy Roubicek emerges as the real Wonder Woman of this psychological struggle. Twenty years later editor Sheldon Mayer was still talking about submarines and trying to make sense of it all.

★   ★   ★

Marston soon had more serious concerns. Around this same time, as World War II was coming to an end, he was diagnosed with infantile paralysis. "He got polio when he was about fifty," said his son Byrne. "He was in a wheelchair the last few years of his life, and that just frustrated him, but he was always productive." His daughter, Olive, recalled the help he received from "another woman, Joye Murchison. Toward the end when Dad was so sick, she helped him out tremendously. Sort of a secretary job."

"My association with Dr. Marston began when I graduated from Katherine Gibbs," said Joye Murchison. "He asked me to work for him as a secretary-writer because I received the highest mark in final exams and would therefore understand his theory behind Wonder Woman." She said her duties increased with the onset of Marston's illness, which she places around 1945, and that she became in effect the co-author of the

75

series. "Scripts were written in play form—some by me, some by Dr. Marston, others together. They were first submitted to Sheldon Mayer for approval. Then the scripts were given to Harry G. Peter and the two women who worked under him. Explicit directions were in the script explaining to the artists exactly what to draw, costumes, the size of panels, backgrounds. The first layouts were done in pencil and checked by me to make sure they followed the script. Then the layouts were inked and sent to the editing offices for final checking and printing."

"When the war is over," Marston had predicted back in 1943 to M. C. Gaines, "I'll show you some developments of Wonder Woman that will make new story strip history!" The comics did move in some different directions, and this was probably owing more to Marston's influence than Joye Murchison's, but Gaines was no longer there to be shown. He and Marston had enjoyed an unusually cordial relationship for a publisher and a writer, as symbolized by each one's donation of his middle name to the pseudonym Charles Moulton, but in 1945 Gaines sold his interest in All American Comics to its sister company, DC Comics. He report-

edly had personality conflicts with DC publisher Harry Donenfeld, and showed good timing by making the sale when wartime paper rationing was in effect and his allotments had short-term value. Sheldon Mayer, now working for DC, continued to edit Wonder Woman so the transition was not too cumbersome.

Relieved of the responsibility to fill his stories with wartime propaganda, Marston felt free to mine the rich vein of fantasy that had always been one of his strengths. Wonder Woman would encounter the gods of Norse myth and the leprechauns of Ireland, and travel through time to defy Puritan witch trials and to meet Marston's old hero Julius Caesar. Marston also continued to populate the solar system with strange civilizations, including an invading army of female "sun warriors" mounted on winged steeds, interplanetary kidnappers from the planet Pluto, and perhaps most memorably, the gorgeous "flying giantesses" known as the "Speed Maniacs from Mercury."

By 1947, Marston was diagnosed with lung cancer. "He kept right on going," according to his son Byrne. "When the morphine got to him he couldn't work, but that wasn't a very long period of time." According to his wife, Elizabeth, Marston "wrote a script the week before he died. Two days before the end he was editing pencils, in writing so faint we could scarcely read it, but catching errors we had passed up." Based on her calculations of the time elapsed between a script and the published comic book, Marston's final story must have been the book-length epic "Villainy Incorporated," in *Wonder Woman* #28 (March–April 1948).

It's a Hollywood cliché to show a revered writer like Charles Dickens or Mark Twain lying on his deathbed while all his beloved characters gather round to bid him farewell. In Marston's case this scene was no fantasy, as he seems to have spent his last days wrapped up in this story, one that had places for a crowd of his favorite creations. Princess Diana was there, of course, along with Etta Candy and the Holliday Girls, but so were no less than eight of Marston's favorite female villains, making one last mass jailbreak from the inadequate Transformation Island. Led by Eviless, a slave driver from the planet Saturn, the team called "Villainy Incorporated" included the Cheetah, Giganta, Queen Clea, Zara of the Crimson Flame Cult, and three wicked women who favored male attire, including Wonder Woman's first female foe, Dr. Poison. Unrepentant to the end, Marston called for seventy-five panels showing women in bondage. And Wonder Woman's mom had the last word: "The only real happiness for anybody is to be found in obedience to loving authority."

William Moulton Marston died on May 2, 1947. Not long after, on August 20, a boating accident claimed the life of M. C. Gaines, the other half of Charles Moulton. Harry Peter and Sheldon Mayer were left to carry on as best they could. "That was the dirtiest trick Marston ever played on me," said Mayer, because when it came to writing Wonder Woman "there was just one right guy, and he had the nerve to die. And he shouldn't have done it."

Marston's remarkable family endured. His children were raised and

A young Byrne Marston was the happy recipient of this handmade Christmas card from Harry Peter. He has held on to it for more than half a century.

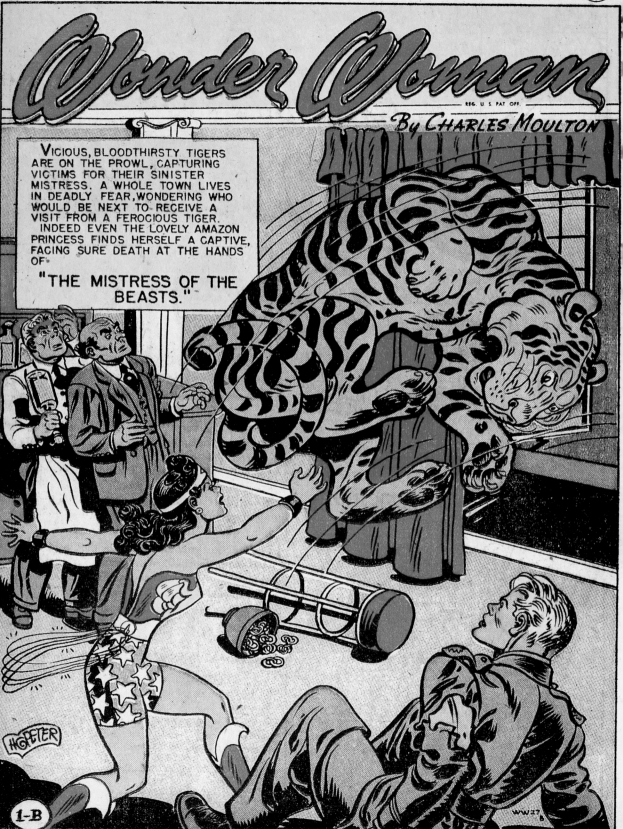

# Wonder Woman

By Charles Moulton

VICIOUS, BLOODTHIRSTY TIGERS ARE ON THE PROWL, CAPTURING VICTIMS FOR THEIR SINISTER MISTRESS. A WHOLE TOWN LIVES IN DEADLY FEAR, WONDERING WHO WOULD BE NEXT TO RECEIVE A VISIT FROM A FEROCIOUS TIGER. INDEED EVEN THE LOVELY AMAZON PRINCESS FINDS HERSELF A CAPTIVE, FACING SURE DEATH AT THE HANDS OF

## "THE MISTRESS OF THE BEASTS."

1-B

Trained animals enforce the demands of an extortion-ist named Tigra Tropica in *Wonder Woman* #26 (November–December 1947).

became successful adults; their mothers, Elizabeth Marston and Olive Richard, the two women who had inspired Wonder Woman, stayed the course. "They really, really thought he was a great man, and they admired him," said Byrne Marston. "Then they had the kids to look after, and Elizabeth kept on until she retired, working at the Metropolitan Life Insurance Company, and my mother, Olive, stayed out in Rye and looked after these four kids. It's kind of crazy, but it worked out and they got along quite well. They were just a pair from then on until they died."

★   ★   ★

After her creator's death, Wonder Woman continued her career with the assistance of writer-editor Robert Kanigher. Although Harry Peter provided some stability as the character's chief artist, Princess Diana was about to embark on a series of changes that would last through Kanigher's twenty-year tenure and beyond. Super heroes were in decline during the period following World War II while other comic book genres like romance achieved new popularity, so Kanigher tried emphasizing the

A 1947 group portrait. Standing left to right: Byrne Marston, Moulton (Pete) Marston, Olive Byrne Richard. Seated left to right: Marjorie Wilkes, Olive Ann Marston, William Moulton Marston, Donn Marston, Elizabeth Holloway Marston.

"Not a sissy in the lot" as the sinister Saturnian Eviless assembles a team of female felons, some in drag, for William Moulton Marston's swan song in *Wonder Woman* #28 (March–April 1948).

relationship between Diana Prince and Steve Trevor; nevertheless, *Sensation Comics* was canceled. Still, in her own comic book Wonder Woman survived the slump and went on to rival the records of Superman and Batman for longevity as a publishing phenomenon.

In 1958, Kanigher introduced the team of penciller Ross Andru and inker Mike Esposito, and their streamlined art style defined the look of the Amazon for a decade. Apparently attempting to attract a younger female audience, stories featured an adolescent version of Princess Diana called Wonder Girl, and then a toddler known as Wonder Tot. Employing editorial sleight-of-hand, Kanigher subsequently arranged for all of them to appear simultaneously, and claimed to be baffled by any confusion among readers. He created goofy villains like the extraterrestrial Glop and the communist Humpty Dumpty called Egg Fu, then banished all his new creations and attempted to revive the style of the 1940s. However, by 1968 both Kanigher and Wonder Woman seemed worn out.

A new era in feminism was dawning at the time, and a radically different interpretation of Wonder Woman emerged through the efforts of writer Dennis O'Neil and artist Mike Sekowsky. Reasoning that readers might appreciate a more realistic figure, they arranged for Wonder Woman to renounce her powers and her costume for a role as a mortal secret agent. Sales improved, but there were protests—most prominently from *Ms.* magazine's Gloria Steinem—that an important symbol of female strength had been subverted; by 1973 Diana Prince was back in her red, white, and blue uniform once more.

Wonder Woman was now established as an icon of the women's movement, but she made her biggest impression on the general public when she got her own television show in 1975. Already on the airwaves as part of an animated team called *Super Friends,* the Amazon was finally embodied by an actress when Lynda Carter took the role in TV movies that soon led to a regular series. Combining statuesque beauty with a down-to-earth demeanor, Carter was an appealing princess whose exploits are still broadcast today.

When DC Comics decided to reinvent all of its characters after a series called *Crisis on Infinite Earths* (1985), writer-artist George Pérez took on the job of jump-starting Wonder Woman. Balancing her essential humanity with her background in ancient myth, Pérez fashioned the template for the modern Amazon, who has since been interpreted by artists as diverse as John Byrne, Brian Bolland, Jill Thompson, and Mike Deodato. In fact, it is the conflicts and tensions in various interpretations of Diana that make her memorable. Invented by men and adopted by women, a role model for girls who was nonetheless designed to win the love of boys, she has a job that only a super hero could fill. Wonder Woman has already had an effect on society that few fictional characters can hope to match. No doubt many adventures lie ahead for her, yet there is a certain satisfaction to be found in realizing how much of her mission has already been accomplished.

Bedwin Footh, named for famed tragedian Edwin Booth (his brother killed Lincoln), is a bad actor but a good excuse for Marston and Peter to bring an all-star cast of villains on stage. From *Sensation Comics* #36 (December 1944).

WONDER WOMAN, FOR THE FIRST TIME IN HER HECTIC CAREER, IS THREATENED BY 6 VILLAINS WHOM SHE HAD PREVIOUSLY CONQUERED! NATURALLY, SHE DREADED THEIR CLEVERNESS - THEIR TREMENDOUS POWER - THEIR KNOWLEDGE OF STRANGE WEAPONS. FAR DOWN IN THE CAVERNS BENEATH A FAMOUS THEATRE, THE GIRL FROM PARADISE ISLAND DEFIES THE COMBINED MENACE OF HER VENGEFUL FOES! SHE OVERCOMES ENORMOUS ODDS BUT IF IT HADN'T BEEN FOR STEVE, THE MIGHTY AMAZON MIGHT HAVE LOST HER "GLITTERING GLAMOUR GIRLS" DESPITE THE MAGNIFICENT BRAVERY OF HER FIGHT.

BEAUTIFUL AS APHRODITE, WISE AS ATHENA, STRONGER THAN HERCULES AND SWIFTER THAN MERCURY, THE PRINCESS OF THE AMAZONS REACHES NEW HEIGHTS OF STUPENDOUS ACHIEVEMENT IN HER "BATTLE AGAINST REVENGE."

A WEIRD AND HAGGARD FACE, CONTORTED WITH BITTER HATRED, STARES MALIGNANTLY AT A PICTURE ON THE FRONT PAGE OF A NEWSPAPER.

ANOTHER PRETTY FOOL THE PUBLIC'S FALLING FOR - THEY'VE FORGOTTEN ME - IDOLIZE HER! BAH! I'LL MAKE HER PAY!

HGPETER

HAH! **SHE** MAKES THE FIRST PAGE WHILE I, **BEDWIN FOOTH**, GREATEST ACTOR OF ALL TIME, MUST HIDE IN THE BOWELS OF THE EARTH, UNKNOWN AND FORGOTTEN! BUT **SHE'LL** PAY ME TRIBUTE - ARRGH! LIKE THE **OTHERS!**

## New York Express EXTRA

THE WEATHER TODAY

VOL. II NO. III          NEW YORK, MARCH 21, 1944

### WONDER WOMAN ON SKATES DRAWS RECORD CROWD AT MADISON SQUARE GARDEN WAR BENEFIT

THE AMAZING AMAZON PRINCESS KNOWN THE WORLD OVER AS WONDER WOMAN, LED HER GLITTERING GLAMOUR GIRLS' ICE BALLET, COMPOSED OF HOLLIDAY COLLEGE GIRLS AND WASHINGTON DEBUTANTES LAST EVENING IN A STARTLING AND BEAUTIFUL PERFORMANCE. WONDER WOMAN PACKED IN THE PAYING CUSTOMERS AND RAISED THE ASTONISHING SUM OF $1,847,568.00 FOR THE DISABLED VETERANS FUND IN A SINGLE EVENING. THE GIRL FROM PARADISE ISLAND WILL REPEAT HER PERFORMANCE TOMORROW

IN MY FILES ARE THE LIFE HISTORIES OF EVERYBODY WHO EVER GOT PUBLICITY - I'LL BREAK 'EM ALL! HM. **WONDER WOMAN'S** DEFEATED **HUNDREDS** OF EVIL DOERS I'LL PICK 6 OF HER MOST POWERFUL ENEMIES!

A - C.

WONDER WOMAN

| NAME | ADDRESS |
| --- | --- |
| DUKE OF DECEPTION | PLANET MARS |
| BLAKFU, KING OF MOLE MEN | MOLE LAND UNDERGROUND |
| DR. PSYCHO | SING SING DEATH CELL |
| THE CHEETAH, PRISCILLA RICH | AMAZON PRISON REFORM ISLAND |
| EX-QUEEN CLEA OF VENTURIA | AURANIAN PRISON, ATLANTIS |
| GIGANTA, THE GORILLA GIRL | IMPRISONED IN PAULA'S SECRET LAB FOR TRAINING |

HAW! HAW! THESE PRETTIES WILL SERVE MY PURPOSE WELL —

2

WONDER WOMAN, LEAVING THE [PLA]CE AT MADISON SQUARE GARDEN [N]EXT EVENING, FINDS STEVE [W]AITING.

ANGEL, YOU WERE MAGNIFICENT!

THANKS, STEVE - BUT WHAT ARE YOU DOING HERE? I THOUGHT YOU WERE CALLED BACK TO WASHINGTON—

COL. DARNELL CALLED ME BACK TO DISCUSS A CONFIDENTIAL TELEGRAM FROM THE WARDEN OF SING SING. BRACE YOURSELF FOR A SHOCK, BEAUTIFUL—

I CAN GUESS YOUR BAD NEWS! DR PSYCHO HAS ESCAPED AGAIN!

THAT'S RIGHT-HOW'D YOU GUESS IT? PSYCHO'S ESCAPED AND- HEY, DON'T PUT ME OUT! I WANT TO TALK—

I'LL SEE YOU LATER, STEVE!

PSYCHO'S DANGEROUS-GREAT HERA! HE CAN MA-TERIALIZE ANY KIND OF BODY FOR DISGUISE, [U]SING HIS WIFE MARVA AS A MEDIUM. SHE'S A WAC [ST]ATIONED IN BOSTON-PSYCHO'LL GO THERE—

JUST A MINUTE-I'M-

RAP RAP RAP

HEY-I TOLD YOU TO WAIT—

PARDON ME LADY-I'M RED FITZ, MANAGER OF THE BOSTON WINTER GARDEN, LOOKING FOR WONDER WOMAN. HM-THERE'S HER CLOTHES- ARE YOU BY ANY CHANCE, WONDER WOMAN IN DISGUISE?

[D]ON'T BE ABSURD! I AM LT. [D]IANA PRINCE OF ARMY INTEL-[L]IGENCE SERVICE!

AH -THEN PERHAPS YOU'VE BEEN WEARING HER CLOTHES! WHERE'S THE REAL WONDER WOMAN?

USING VENTRILOQUISM, DIANA DIVERTS HER VISITOR'S ATTENTION WHILE SHE MAKES A LIGHTNING CHANGE OF PERSONALITY.

HERE I AM!

WHERE-WHAT- SAY, AM I NUTS- WHERE ARE YOU?

RIGHT HERE, MR. FITZ!

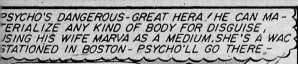

I'M GLAD TO MEET YOU, SIR!

OUCH - OWW, MY HAND! YOU'RE THE **REAL WONDER WOMAN**, BEYOND DOUBT!

BOSTON NEEDS YOU, **WONDER WOMAN!** BRING YOUR GIRLS TO MY WINTER GARDEN AND GIVE **US** A BENEFIT PERFORMANCE!

AS DIANA PRINCE, I OUGHT TO BE IN WASHINGTON - BUT IN BOSTON, I MIGHT CATCH PSYCHO -

VERY WELL - I'LL ACCEPT YOUR INVITATION!

OH - AH - EXCUSE ME FROM SHAKING HANDS - YOUR GRIP IS SO - ER - OVERWHELMING! I'LL SEE YOU IN BOSTON.

OKAY - I'LL RUN UP TOMORROW, NEED THE EXERCISE! MY GIRLS WILL FOLLOW BY TRAIN -

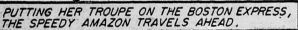

PUTTING HER TROUPE ON THE BOSTON EXPRESS, THE SPEEDY AMAZON TRAVELS AHEAD.

BYE, **WONDER WOMAN!**

WOO WOO, THAT BABE CAN TROT! SEE YOU AT THE WINTER GARDEN BOSS!

AT THE BIG BOSTON THEATRE, AN EXCITED GIRL WAITS FOR **WONDER WOMAN.**

I'M MARVA, DR. PSYCHO'S WIFE - REMEMBER ME? HE'S ESCAPED - PLEASE COME WITH ME --

NOT NOW, MARVA - THE SHOW MUST COME FIRST - BUT DON'T WORRY - I'VE A PLAN TO CATCH PSYCHO!

TONIGHT "WINTER GARDEN" PRESENTS *Wonder Woman* IN ARMY BENEFIT

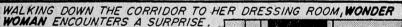

WALKING DOWN THE CORRIDOR TO HER DRESSING ROOM, **WONDER WOMAN** ENCOUNTERS A SURPRISE.

GREAT MINERVA - THE CHEETAH!

ARR - RRGH! MY EVIL PERSONALITY RULED TRIUMPHANT UNTIL **YOU** DISCOVERED I'M PRISCILLA RICH AND PUT ME IN PRISON - NOW I'LL GET **REVENGE!**

I'LL SOON HAVE YOU BACK ON REFORM ISLAND, MY FEROCIOUS FRIEND!

4

WELL, I'LL BE A KANGA'S UNCLE! THE CHEETAH CERTAINLY CAME IN HERE BUT THE ROOM'S EMPTY—MAYBE I **DREAMED** I SAW HER!!

AS **WONDER WOMAN**, BAFFLED, RETURNS TO THE CORRIDOR, SHE IS CONFRONTED BY ANOTHER ENEMY.

I **AM** SEEING THINGS-QUEEN CLEA OF LOST ATLANTIS!

I RULED MY CONTINENT WITH THE SWORD UNTIL **THOU** STOPPED ME—I'LL HAVE REVENGE!

SLAM!

THE GIRL FROM PARADISE ISLAND THROWS HER LASSO A SPLIT SECOND TOO LATE.

HMP— MISSED HER! THE SURPRISE OF SEEING THESE OLD FRIENDS MUST BE SLOWING ME UP!

SLAM!

CLEA OUGHT TO KNOW THAT A LOCKED DOOR WON'T STOP AN ATLANTEAN GIRL—NOR AN AMAZON!

BUT AGAIN **WONDER WOMAN** FINDS HERSELF ALONE IN AN EMPTY ROOM.

CLEA'S DISAPPEARED! I'D THINK SEEING HER HERE WAS AN ILLUSION BUT **SOMEBODY** LOCKED THAT DOOR!

COMPLETELY BEWILDERED BY THIS STRANGE SERIES OF EVENTS, THE AMAZON GIRL FINDS A STILL GREATER SURPRISE AWAITING HER.

GREAT APHRODITE—THE DUKE OF DECEPTION FROM MARS AND GIGANTA, THE GORILLA GIRL! AM I HYPNOTIZED OR **ASLEEP**? I'LL PINCH MYSELF—

⑤

YOU SMASHED MY SPACE CRUISER, **WONDER WOMAN**, AND SENT ME BACK TO DISGRACE AND CHAINS ON MARS! I'VE COME TO EARTH FOR **REVENGE**!

HA—**WONDER WOMAN**! YOU CAPTURED ME WHEN I WAS A GORILLA—WHEN PROF. ZOOL'S EVOLUTION MACHINE MADE ME A CAVE GIRL, YOU CONQUERED ME AGAIN. BUT I'LL GET **REVENGE**!

WONDER WOMAN, UNCERTAIN HOW TO ACT, HESITATES TOO LONG AND—

AH-BAH! ANOTHER MISS—

HA! HA! HA! HA!

AS I EXPECTED—THEY'VE **BOTH** DISAPPEARED! I'D THINK THESE WERE ECTOPLASMIC BODIES MATERIALIZED BY PSYCHO EXCEPT THAT MARVA, HIS MEDIUM, IS FREE—DR. PSYCHO CAN'T DO HIS TRICKS UNLESS MARVA'S BOUND IN A TRANCE!

IN HER DRESSING ROOM, **WONDER WOMAN** TAKES PRECAUTIONS.

IF MY ENEMIES CAPTURE ME, THEY'LL TRY TO BIND ME WITH MY MAGIC LASSO. BUT I'LL FOOL THEM—THIS WAY IT'LL LOOK LIKE A SOLID GOLD AMULET!

**WONDER WOMAN**, READY TO DON HER SKATES, RECEIVES AN AMAZING VISITOR.

WELL, **THIS** IS THE PAY-OFF—IT'S BLAKFU, KING OF THE MOLE MEN!

I'VE COME TO **HELP** YOU, **WONDER WOMAN!**

YOU CONQUERED MY UNDERGROUND KINGDOM AND FREED OUR SLAVES—BUT YOU RESTORED THE SIGHT OF US BLIND MOLEMEN, SO I'M YOUR FRIEND. I'M HERE TO HELP YOU!

HM—I WONDER! HOW CAN YOU HELP?

YOUR ENEMIES ARE HIDING IN SECRET CAVERNS BENEATH THIS THEATRE. I KNOW THE DEPTHS OF THE EARTH AND I'LL TAKE YOU THERE. WHEN I PRESS THIS SWITCH, A HIDDEN DOOR OPENS—

HO HO! YOU STOPPED ME FROM CONQUERING THE EARTH, **WONDER WOMAN**—THIS IS MY REVENGE!

DOWN PLUNGES WONDER WOMAN INTO UNKNOWN DEPTHS. BLAKFU KEPT HIS WORD—HE'S TAKING ME TO MY ENEMIES BY THE SHORTEST ROUTE!

WONDER WOMAN IS CAUGHT IN A NET AND SUSPENDED OVER SHARP STEEL SPIKES.

HA HA HA! HO HA! REVENGE IS SWEET!

SURRENDER, AMAZON! LOOK DOWN—YOU'LL SEE THE POINT!

THERE'S MORE THAN ONE POINT TO BE CONSIDERED—WHAT'S THIS GAG ALL ABOUT?

I AM BEDWIN FOOTH, GREATEST ACTOR EVER IGNORED BY A STUPID PUBLIC! BUT THE STAGE'S LOSS IS THE UNDERWORLD'S GAIN—MY CRIME STOCK COMPANY IS INCOMPARABLE! YOU SHALL JOIN IT AND RECEIVE MY TRAINING!

YOU'RE CRAZY, PAL!

⑦

DIE, THEN, VAIN BUTTERFLY, WHO SPURNS FOOTH, COURTS DEATH!

AS SHE STARTS TO FALL TOWARD THE DEADLY SPIKES, THE MIGHTY AMAZON BURSTS HER NET AND TURNS HEAD DOWNWARD.

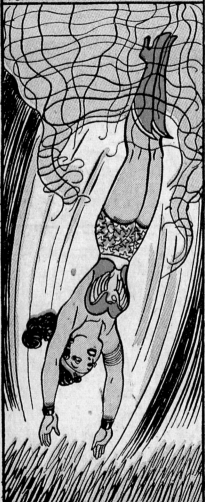

GRASPING TWO SPIKES BELOW THEIR POINTS **WONDER WOMAN** BREAKS HER FALL.

PERFECTLY POISED, THE AMAZON GIRL WALKS A SPIKED PATH WITH HER HANDS.

AS **WONDER WOMAN** FLIPS UPWARD TO HER FEET, FOOTH'S "CRIMINAL STOCK COMPANY" FLEE IN TERROR.

SHE—SHE'S SUPERHUMAN! RUN QUICK—THE BACK PASSAGE!

WAIT—I THOUGHT YOU WANTED ME TO JOIN YOUR COMPANY!

AS **WONDER WOMAN** LEAPS AFTER THE FUGITIVES A HUGE BOULDER IS RELEASED BY A SECRET MECHANISM.

WITH THE SWIFTNESS OF MERCURY AND THE STRENGTH OF HERCULES, **WONDER WOMAN** CATCHES THE ENORMOUS ROCK IN HER HANDS.

HOW ANNOYING—WHILE I STOP TO PLAY WITH THIS LITTLE STONE, FOOTH'S GANG IS ESCAPING.

8

THE PASSAGE REACHES A DEAD END.

HMPH—MY CRIME COMRADES HAVE DISAPPEARED AGAIN! THIS LAD-DER MAY LEAD TO THE THEATRE ABOVE—

SCALING THE LADDER SWIFTLY, **WONDER WOMAN** FINDS A MAS-SIVE METAL DOOR.

SORRY BUT I HAVEN'T TIME TO FIND THE SECRET CATCH ON THIS DOOR—

LEAPING THROUGH THE OPENING, **WONDER WOMAN** FINDS HERSELF IN MANAGER FITZ'S OFFICE.

YE GODS—**WONDER WOMAN!** WHERE'VE YOU BEEN? YOUR GIRLS ARE IN TERRIBLE DAN-GER—ONLY **YOU** CAN SAVE THEM!

MEANWHILE, THE GIRLS ARRIVE AND LINE UP FOR PRACTICE.

WHERE'S **WONDER WOMAN?** WE NEED HER TO DIRECT US—

SHE PROB'LY FORGOT WHERE BOSTON IS AND WENT ON RUN-NIN'! BUT DON'T WORRY, **I'LL** DIRECT YOU!

FIRST I'LL SHOW YOU HOW TO DO A DUET WHIRL LIKE THIS— OOOF—OUCH!

BAM

SUDDENLY, MARVA, IN SKATING COSTUME, GLIDES GRACEFULLY TOWARD THE GIRLS.

HELLO, GIRLS—HOW D'YOU LIKE THIS **BOSTON GLIDE?**

SWELL, KEED, SHOW US SOME MORE FANCY STUFF!

MARVA SURPRISES THE VISITORS WITH HER SKILLFUL SKATING.

HERE'S THE "FLYING VIENNESE"—WHY NOT PRACTICE IT FOR YOUR SHOW?

⑨

LET ME SHOW YOU GIRLS AN INTERESTING GROUP ROUTINE!

YES, YES— WE'D LOVE TO LEARN IT!

THIS ACT IS CALLED "SKATING ON THE CEILING". THERE'S A TRICK CEILING HERE. I'LL HAVE IT LOWERED— **DON'T** CHANGE YOUR POSITIONS!

A GREAT METALLIC PLATE LOWERED FROM ABOVE, ATTRACTS THE GIRLS' SKATES MAGNETICALLY AS IT APPROACHES THEM.

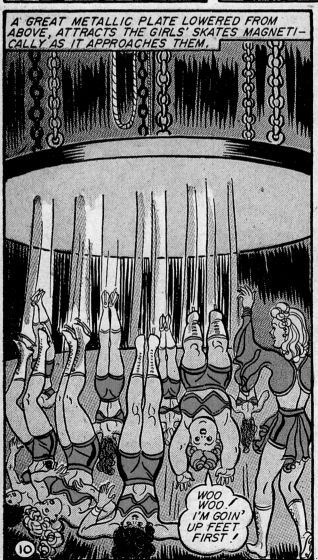

WOO WOO! I'M GOIN' UP FEET FIRST!

10

THE "TRICK CEILING" MOVES UP AGAIN, SUSPENDING THE GIRLS BY THEIR MAGNETICALLY HELD SKATES.

HEY! LET US DOWN!

HA HA HA!! STANDING ON YOUR HEAD IS GOOD FOR YOU! THE HINDUS SAY IT IMPROVES YOUR BRAINS!!

MANAGER RED FITZ SHOWS **WONDER WOMAN** AN AMAZING SCENE.

YOUR FORMER ENEMIES HAVE CAPTURED YOUR GIRLS, **WONDER WOMAN**—THEY DEMAND YOUR SURRENDER OR THE GIRLS DIE!

THEY—THEY'RE CLEVER—I—I SUPPOSE I MUST—SURRENDER!

GIVE ME YOUR MAGIC LASSO TO BIND YOUR HANDS—THEN THEY'LL FREE YOUR GIRLS.

HM—YOU SEEM TO KNOW A LOT ABOUT HOW TO BIND ME—I **HID** MY LASSO!

**EVERYBODY** KNOWS ABOUT YOU, **WONDER WOMAN**—I ER—HAVE TO SATISFY THESE CRIMINALS TO SAVE YOUR GIRLS, I'LL CHAIN YOUR AMAZON BRACELETS TOGETHER!

VERY WELL— I SUBMIT!

WHEN YOUR SUPER-STRENGTH IS TAKEN AWAY YOU'LL JOIN THE CRIME STOCK COMPANY OR—

PLUTO'S PUNISHMENTS! WHAT DO **YOU** KNOW ABOUT FOOTH'S CRIME GANG?

WAIT A MINUTE—BEFORE I SURRENDER MY APHRODITE-GIVEN STRENGTH—OOGA—WOOGMA—WUMP! AREAR FUMPO SWIOP! UNGAR DEEPRA DOON! BY HERCULES! THE APE GIRL, DECEPTION AND THE MOLEMAN KING DON'T UNDERSTAND A WORD OF THEIR NATIVE LANGUAGES!

WHIPPING OUT AN AUTOMATIC, FITZ REVEALS HIS TRUE CHARACTER.

MAYBE THOSE BLOKES AND THEIR FANCY WEAPONS **ARE** FAKES—BUT MY **GUN** AND CLEA'S **SWORD** WILL FINISH YOUR GIRLS IN SPLIT SECONDS UNLESS YOU SUBMIT TO BONDS!

**WONDER WOMAN** LEAPS SWIFTLY TO PROTECT HER GIRLS.

I BEGIN TO SEE THE SECRET OF THIS DEVILTRY—COME ON, PARTNERS, LET'S HAVE FUN!

THIS DAME'S SUPER-HUMAN—SHE'S GOT THE STRENGTH OF TEN DEVILS!

STEVE, MEANWHILE, CALLS SING SING PRISON.

HELLO, WARDEN—TELL ME HOW DR. PSYCHO ESCAPED—

PSYCHO—**ESCAPED?** YOU'RE MISINFORMED, MAJOR! HE'S SAFELY IN HIS DEATH CELL AND WE'LL KEEP HIM THERE UNTIL THE EXECUTION DATE!

I TOLD **WONDER WOMAN** PSYCHO HAD ESCAPED AND SHE WENT TO BOSTON—PROBABLY TO DISCOVER MARVA, PSYCHO'S WIFE. SOMEONE SENT A PHONY TELEGRAM, KNOWING I'D TELL **WONDER WOMAN.** THEY'RE TRYING TO TRAP HER! I MUST REACH MY ANGEL BEFORE THEY GET HER—

STEVE RUSHES TO BOSTON IN A HELICOPTER, LANDING ON THE WINTER GARDEN ROOF.

THE ARMY INTELLIGENCE ACE CRASHES THROUGH THE THEATRE SKY-LIGHT.

THIS IS THE QUICKEST WAY INTO THE THEATRE. MINUTES MAY MEAN **WONDER WOMAN'S** LIFE.

STEVE ARRIVES IN THE NICK OF TIME—WHILE **WONDER WOMAN** REPULSES TWO ENEMIES, THE OTHERS MENACE HER HELPLESS GIRLS.

THAT'S A MAGNET HOLDING THOSE GIRLS' SKATES! I'LL SHOOT THE ELECTRIC WIRE THAT SUPPLIES THE MAGNETIC POWER—

WITH EXPERT MARKSMANSHIP, STEVE'S BULLET SEVERS THE ELECTRIC MAGNETS' SUPPLY WIRE.

THE GIRLS, THEIR SKATES RELEASED FROM THE DEAD MAGNET, DROP TO THE ICE.

**WONDER WOMAN** AND HER GIRLS SWIFTLY DISPOSE OF THEIR ADVERSARIES!

IF YOU'RE GIGANTA, I'M FERDINAND THE BULL!

SWIFTLY STRIPPING THE MAGIC LASSO FROM HER ARM, **WONDER WOMAN** CAPTURES AND UN-MASKS "RED FITZ," THE DUAL-PERSONALITY WINTER-GARDEN MANAGER.

YOU'RE BEDWIN FOOTH!

Y-YES-S-SOMETHING COMPELS ME TO C-CONFESS!

I TELEGRAPHED TREVOR THAT PSYCHO HAD ESCAPED. THESE "ENEMIES OF **WONDER WOMAN**" ARE ACTORS I CONTROL! FOR 30 YEARS, I'VE LIVED IN CAVERNS BENEATH THIS THEATRE, CAPTURING SUCCESSFUL PLAYERS AND MAKING THEM JOIN MY UNDERWORLD CRIME COMPANY!

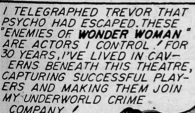

A FORMER STAR ACTRESS AND SKATER PLAYED "MARVA"—SHE FAILED TO TRAP WONDER WOMAN BUT GOT HER GIRLS THE REST YOU KNOW!

YOU BELONG IN AN IN-SANE ASYLUM, MY FRIEND!

THAT WAS NICE SHOOTING, STEVE! —YOU'RE AN EXCELLENT MARKSMAN——

I WON'T CALL MYSELF A MARKSMAN TILL I MAKE A HIT WITH YOU --- ALL RIGHT, SO YOU WON'T MARRY ME— BUT HOW ABOUT A DATE?

# ACKNOWLEDGMENTS

Like an army of Amazons descending on a helpless pile of paper, countless people have conspired to produce this book. Thanks to designer Chip Kidd for consolidating an infinite array of images into such a pleasing package, photographer Geoff Spear for transforming tiny toys into mesmerizing monuments, design assistant Chin-Yee Lai for making sure the whole jigsaw puzzle fit together, artist Alex Ross for his heroic cover illustration, and Steve Korté, an outstanding editor whose invaluable input invariably transcends his job description.

A series of generously granted interviews made the text possible, and special gratitude must be extended to the children of Wonder Woman's creator: Byrne Marston, Pete Marston, and Olive Marston LaMotte. Our appreciation also to Edgar May, who put us in touch with the Marston family. And thanks for the memories to Irwin Hasen and Jack Liebowitz.

Collectors, creators, and critics contributed to the cause. DC librarian Allan Asherman once again unearthed a treasure trove of precious newsprint, and Marc Witz unerringly shot the emerging images. Alice Cloos allowed us to photograph her spectacular collection of Amazonian artifacts, Rob Stolzer supplied us with early Harry Peter art, and Leslie Overstreet opened the Smithsonian. The Mad Peck Studio Archives continued to constitute a cornucopia, and further invaluable assistance was provided by Steve Ahlquist, Dave Anderson, Jerry Bails, Bill Blackbeard, Mike Chandley, Jon B. Cooke, Grant Geissman, Ron Goulart, Marty Greim, Alan Holtz, Richard Howell, Peter Kiefer, Ray Kelly, Matt Larson, Will Murray, Rick Roe, Randy Scott, Kirk Stark, Maggie Thompson, and Robert Colleson.

At Chronicle Books, this project was aided and abetted by Sarah Malarkey, Beth Weber, Anne Bunn, Sara Schneider, Julia Flagg, Michael Carabetta, Steve Moore, and Shona Bayley. And at Writers House, my agent Merrilee Heifetz remains unconquerable.

At DC, for assistance above and beyond the call of duty, a tip of the tiara to Lourdes Arocho, Ed Bolkus, Georg Brewer, Mark Chiarello, Dorothy Crouch, Dale Crain, Marilyn Drucker, Trent Duffy, Larry Ganem, Jaye Gardner, Charles Kochman, Jay Kogan, Lillian Laserson, Sandy Resnick, Rich Thomas, and Jeanette Winley. Paul Levitz and Mark Waid each gave the manuscript an expert once-over, and Mike Tiefenbacher checked the art credits, but they should not be held responsible for any possible errors.

And finally, this book is fondly dedicated to my wonderful friend Fiona, who will

# INDEX

*All American Comics* (comic book), 20, 27
*All American Comics* (company), 20, 25, 30, 39, 40, 41, 65, 67, 76
*All Star Comics* (comic book), 30, 33, 52, 55
Amazons, 21, 26, 31, 37, 39, 60–61, 63
*American Scholar, The,* 11
Andru, Ross, 80
Aphrodite, 27, 31, 42
Armer, Frank, 18
*Art of Sound Pictures, The* (Marston and Pitkin), 18, 22
"Astounding Adventures of Olga Mesmer, the Girl with the X-Ray Eyes," 18
Atom, the, 55

"Baby party," 17, 20, 31, 37
Bails, Jerry, 13
Baker, Matt, 52
Batman, 25, 35, 40, 54, 55, 80
Bender, Dr. Lauretta, 68, 74
Binder, Otto, 40
Blackbeard, Bill, 54
Black Canary, 40
Bolland, Brian, 80
Bondage, 17, 25, 61–75, 77
Boston University, 13
*Boy Commandos,* 40
"Bullets and Bracelets," 31
Bunn, Geoffrey C., 16
Byrne, John, 80
Byrne, Olive, 17
  *see also* Richard, Olive

Caesar, Julius, 17, 77
Cameron, Don, 40
Candy, Etta, 37, 77
*Captive Wild Woman,* 61
Captivity, 61–63, 65
Carter, Lynda, 80
Censorship, 63–75
Cheetah, the, 55, 60, 77
Clea, Queen, 61, 77
Columbia University, 20
Comic books, 11–12, 20, 23
*Comic Cavalcade,* 52
*Crisis on Infinite Earths,* 80

DC Comics, 18, 20, 25, 30, 40, 67, 76–77
Deodato, Mike, Jr., 80
Dick Tracy, 25
Dr. Poison, 36, 37, 77
Dr. Psycho, 54–55
Dominance, 16
Donenfeld, Harry, 18, 20, 77
"Don't Laugh at the Comics," 23

EC Comics, 20
Egg Fu, 80
"Elementary behavior units," 16, 17–18
*Emotions of Normal People* (Marston), 16, 69–72
Erotic fantasies, 74
Erotic love, 22
Esposito, Mike, 80
Ethnic stereotypes, 41–42
Eviless, 77

*Family Circle, The,* 23, 31
Feldstein, Al, 52
Feminist movement, 21, 22, 35, 80
*F. F. Proctor: Vaudeville Pioneer* (Marston), 21
Fiction House, 52
Fisher, Bud, 23, 27, 28
Flash, the, 20, 55
*Flash Comics,* 20, 40
Fox, Gardner, 55
Fox, Victor, 52
Fox Features, 52
Frank, Josette, 63–65, 66–68, 74
Freud, Sigmund, 16

Gaines, Maxwell Charles, 20, 23–25, 27, 52, 76–77
  censorship issue and, 63–67, 68–72
Gaines, William, 20, 45
*Gearshifters,* 54
Gibson, Charles Dana, 28
Giganta, 61, 77
Gillette razor blades, 21
Glop, the, 80
"Good girl art," 52
Gould, Chester, 25
Great Depression, 20
Green Lantern, 20, 37, 55

Harvard University, 13
Hawkman, 20, 40, 55
Herbert, Hugh, 37
Holliday Girls, 37, 77
*Hunchback of Notre Dame, The,* 18–20

Infantino, Carmine, 40
*Integrative Psychology: A Study of Unit Response* (Marston et al.), 21

Jackson College, 17
*Journal of Experimental Psychology, The,* 16
*Judge,* 28
*Jumbo Comics,* 52
*Jungle Comics,* 52
Justice Society of America, 20, 30, 40, 52, 55

Kamen, Jack, 52
Kanigher, Robert, 40, 79–80
King, C. Daly, 21
King Features, 52
Kleinbaum, Abby Wettan, 21

Liberty Belle, 41
Liebowitz, Jack, 11, 18, 20
Lie detectors, 12–13, 16, 49
*Lie Detector Test, The* (Marston), 21

McClure newspaper syndicate, 20
Mala, 31, 38, 39
Marble, Alice, 41
*March On* (Marston), 21, 22
Mars, war god (Aries), 42–45
Marston, Byrne, 16, 20, 21, 31–33, 45, 46, 50, 75, 77, 79
Marston, Donn Richard, 31–33, 46
Marston, Elizabeth Holloway, 13, 21–22, 31, 33, 49, 77, 79
Marston, Fredericka, 33, 46
Marston, Louise, 50
Marston, Moulton "Pete," 31, 45, 49
Marston, Olive Ann, 31, 46, 50, 75, 76
Marston, William Moulton, 11–33, 35, 37, 38, 41, 45
  censorship issue, 63–75
  creative process of, 26
  death of, 77
  described, 46
  illnesses of, 75, 77
  interest in comics, 11–12, 23
  last days of, 77
  lie detectors and, 12–13, 16
  pen name of, 26, 39
  psychic phenomena and, 55
  "psychological propaganda," 52–54
  psychological theories of, 16, 17–18, 18, 21
  as published author, 11–12, 16–17, 18, 21
  revealed as author of Wonder Woman, 39
  as teacher, 20
  unusual family arrangement of, 31–33
Marston Art Studio, 49–50
Marston family, 31–33, 46, 49–50, 77–79
Mayer, Sheldon, 25–26, 27–28, 33, 35, 39–40, 63, 75, 76, 77
  Marston family and, 46–49
Merry, the Girl of a Thousand Gimmicks, 40
Moulton, Charles (pseud.), *see* Marston, William Moulton
*Ms.,* 80
Münsterberg, Hugo, 13–16
Murchison, Joye, 75–76
"Mutt and Jeff," 20, 23, 27

*New York Journal-American,* 54
*New York Times, The,* 17, 22
New York University, 20
*New York World-Telegram,* 17

O'Neil, Dennis, 80

Paradise Island, 30, 65, 67
Pérez, George, 80
Personalities of blondes, brunettes, and redheads, 17–18
Peter, Harry, 27–28, 41, 52, 76, 77, 79
  described, 49–50
Phantom Lady, 52
Pitkin, Walter B., 18
*Planet Comics,* 52
Plastic Man, 37
*Private Life of Julius Caesar, The* (Marston), 17

Quality Comics, 52

Radcliffe College, 20

*Reader's Digest,* 21
Red Tornado, 20
Richard, Olive, 23, 31–33, 79
  *see also* Byrne, Olive
*Rio Rita,* 18
Roubicek, Dorothy, 65–66, 68, 74–75

Sadism, 67, 68
Schepens, Helen, 50
"Scribbly," 20
Sekowsky, Mike, 80
*Sensation Comics,* 33, 36, 37, 41, 52, 74, 80
Sheena, Queen of the Jungle, 52
*Show Boat,* 18
Shuster, Joe, 23
Siegel, Jerry, 23, 40
Sones, W. W. D., 68, 69
*Spicy Detective Stories,* 18
*Spicy Mystery Stories,* 18
*Star Spangled Comics,* 40
Steinem, Gloria, 80
Stelling, Helen Wainwright, 41
Submission, 16, 18, 22, 38, 67, 68, 72
*Super Friends,* 80
Super heroes, 79, 80
Superman, 20, 23–25, 35, 40, 45, 54, 55, 80
"Systolic Blood Pressure Symptoms of Deception" (Marston), 16

*Tales from the Crypt,* 45
Thompson, Jill, 80
Transformation Island, 38–39, 55, 77
Trevor, Steve, 30, 36, 40
*Try Living* (Marston), 21
Tufts University, 20, 31

U.S. Army, 72
Universal Pictures, 18–20
University of Southern California, 20
Utopian philosophy, 22–23

"Venus girdle," 38, 63
*Venus with Us* (Marston), 17, 21
"Villainy Incorporated," 77
Violence, repudiation of, 23, 31, 45
Von Gunther, Baroness Paula, 37–39, 41

Waugh, Coulton, 26
Wheeler-Nicholson, Major Malcolm, 18
*Who's Who,* 33
Wilkes, Marjorie, 50
Winter, Chuck, 40
Women's domination over men, 22, 26–27
Women's liberation, 22
Wonder Girl, 80
Wonder Tot, 80
Wonder Woman:
  allies of, 37, 41
  as an inspiring figure, 41
  background information about, 39–40
  bondage issue and, 61–75
  bracelets of, 31, 33, 63
  cartoonist who first drew, 27–28
  code card, 45
  costume of, 65–66
  creation of, 23–27
  debut of, 28–30, 55
  as Diana Prince or Princess Diana, 30, 31, 33, 35–36, 41, 77, 80
  dual role of, 11, 35–36
  as emblem of feminism, 80
  fantasy themes, 77
  golden lasso of, 13, 40, 63
  inspiration for, 33
  invisible plane of, 40
  Justice Society of America, 55
  male readership of, 35
  Marston and, *see* Marston, William Moulton
  "mental radio" of, 37
  newspaper strip, 52–54
  original name of, 27
  post–Golden Age developments, 79–80
  script changes, 45
  TV versions of, 80
  villains and, *see specific villains*
*Wonder Woman* comic book, 42–45, 54, 74, 77
  circulation, 52
  first issue of, 39, 41
"Wonder Women of History," 41
World War II, 30, 35–36, 37, 40, 55, 75, 76–77

*You Can Be Popular* (Marston), 21

Zara of the Crimson Flame Cult, 77